Homoeopathic Therapeutics in Ophthalmology

John L. Moffat

Alpha Editions

This edition published in 2019

ISBN : 9789353864347

Design and Setting By
Alpha Editions
email - alphaedis@gmail.com

Homœopathic Therapeutics

IN

Ophthalmology

BY

JOHN L. MOFFAT, B.S., M.D., O. et A. Chir.

President, 1902, Homœopathic Medical Society of the State of New York; Vice-President, 1905 and 1908, American Homœopathic Ophthalmological, Otological and Laryngological Society; Ophthalmic Surgeon, 1894-1911, Cumberland Street Hospital, New York; Contributor to the American Encyclopedia and Dictionary of Ophthalmology.

PHILADELPHIA
BOERICKE & TAFEL
1916

5

DEDICATED

TO MY BROTHER

EDGAR V. MOFFAT, A.M., M.D., O. et A. Chir.

OF ORANGE, N. J.

PREFACE.

Ophthalmological literature is increasing so rapidly, as are the advances in pathology, surgery, physiology and anatomy, that books on those subjects soon become behind the times. Hence monographs are among the most valuable elements of an up to date library, largely because they do not waste shelf room by the repetition deemed essential in text books or by the necessity of retaining a book only a portion of which remains up to date.

For this reason, and because it is generally recognized now that many eye cases require for their cure constitutional, internal, medication rather than or supplemented by local or surgical treatment, the author has confined himself to the facts of our homœopathic materia medica, the pathogenetic symptoms of drugs and clinical experience of their curative action. These will be of practical value generations hence, as they are now and have been for generations in the past.

The systematic arrangement of the materia medica will facilitate ready reference. Drug characteristics are given because with their aid a much more successful prescription may be made.

This book is small, the remedies comparatively few, because only reliable indications have been given. Quality has been preferred to quantity. To most of the remedies in our materia medica have there been attributed one or more eye symptoms but, as yet, without confirmation. To include these would but serve to confuse the reader and impair his confidence.

The following pages are offered to the ophthalmologists who, in increasing numbers, are turning to homœopathy for therapeutic help. But play fair, please. Do not condemn homœopathy if your experiments in empiricism fail. Choosing a remedy from the repertory for a disease or a symptom is empiricism, not homœopathy! Make sincere efforts at individualization and symptom-similarity. A succession of remedies as indicated may be necessary for a cure, as the rungs of a ladder have to be surmounted successively. And failure is more apt to mean a shortcoming on the part of the prescriber than of homœopathy. Homœopathic prescribing is not easy; it is the long way around. But, oh, the joy of a really homœopathic cure! That is to be experienced to be appreciated.

With such personal notes as each owner may make of new symptoms, verifications and clinical results clearly attributable to the single remedy it is hoped that this volume may become a cherished handbook throughout the owner's practice and even (as is the case with more than one book in the author's own library) for a second generation.

Ithaca, N. Y., 1916.

TABLE OF CONTENTS.

CHAPTER I.

CHAPTER II.

CHAPTER III.

CHAPTER IV.

Homœopathic Therapeutics IN Ophthalmology.

CHAPTER I.

HAHNEMANN.

Hofrat Samuel Hahnemann (1755-1843), M. D., Erlangen, 1779, should be—eventually will be—classed with Hippocrates. As Hippocrates brought diseases within the category of classifiable phenomena, so Hahnemann brought drug action within the category of scientific phenomena. He was the first to parallel medicinal with pathognomonic effects, artificial drug diseases with actual human disease, and scientifically, systematically, to study the action of drugs upon the human body.

Hahnemann demonstrated that drugs produce in the healthy body diseases like natural diseases except that the drug disease ceases when the drug is stopped.

Hahnemann was not the first to declare that likes may be cured with likes (Hippocrates enunciated this) nor was he the first to try the effect of drugs upon the healthy—Stoerck did this in 1760—and Haller was the first to suggest that if we wish to know the action of drugs they should be administered separately. But to Hahnemann is due the credit of creating and building up a therapeutic system of cure by symptom-similarity based upon drug provings on the healthy. He alone possessed the requisite medical, chemical and literary knowledge, the scientific insight and thoroughness, the perseverance and the intellect to grasp the subject in mass and detail, that were necessary for the development of what had been but a vague idea in the minds of others.

A master of ancient literature and of nine languages (besides a smattering of Chaldaic), Hahnemann was a prominent chemist and physician, well known beyond the borders of his own country for his masterly translations and discoveries in chemistry; he possessed distinguished friends and patients of high position in the medical profession and among the reigning nobility. Ahead of his times, a pioneer in sanitation and in the humane treatment of insanity,* he became so disgusted with the errors, uncertainties, confusion and failures of medicine that he gave up practice shortly after his marriage

*Antedating Pinel.

and supported his family by translating; later he resumed practice when far enough advanced to do so homœopathically.

In 1790, while translating Cullen's Materia Medica, he was led to experiment upon himself with Peruvian bark, to study its effects upon a person in health, and demonstrated that it could produce the same phenomena (symptoms) as those of ague, which disease it had a reputation of curing. This led to testing other drugs upon himself and many friends; he verified his observations by ransacking the materia medica for recorded experiments and the whole history of poisoning. Six years were thus spent and then he published in the leading medical periodical of the day* his "Essay on a New Principle for Discovering the Curative Power of Drugs."

The necessity of preparing his own medicines incited the enmity of the pharmacists, who formed a very powerful guild. Then the physicians turned a cold shoulder upon his reforms and ostracised him. Finally he moved to Paris where he enjoyed an immense lucrative practice and died in 1843, full of honors, at the age of eighty-eight.

---

*Hufeland's *Journal der praktischen Arzeneikunde und Wundarzeneikunst*, 1796. Vol. II, parts 3 and 4.

CHAPTER II.

HOMŒOPATHY.

Hahnemann taught that all cases of constitutional disease that are curable with medicine will be cured by the administration of that which has the power to cause similar symptoms in the healthy body—*homœopathy.** He also recognized two other methods of medicinal treatment: *antipathy,* the palliative method of symptom-contrariety, and *allopathy,* symptom-dissimilarity, the digressive or eliminative method. But these are not so satisfactory; they are not scientific or thoroughly curative. The latter particularly is based upon the *interpretation* of the observed phenomena.

Facts are permanent and speak for themselves; their explanations will necessarily change with our conceptions of pathology.

While emphasizing that theory and explanation are entirely secondary in importance to observed facts, Hahnemann proffered a vitalistic explanation of how the homœopathic remedy

*"Organon of Rational Healing;" first published in 1810. His fifth edition appeared in 1833; this has been translated 15 times (21 editions) into French, English, Russian, Spanish, Italian, Hungarian and Swedish, and in 1913 a new translation of the first edition was published in "Everyman's Library."

cures. Observing that nature, at times, cures by the advent of a stronger *similar* disease, Hahnemann asserted that homœopathy is the natural way to cure: that the drug disease, if similar in its manifestations (symptoms), carries off the patient's disease with it as it passes off; hence the name homœopathy from, ὅμοιον *homoion*, like or similar, and παζος *pathos*, disease or affection. He perceived that we can have actual knowledge only of phenomena (facts); that we can recognize disease only by its phenomena (its symptoms, subjective and objective), that hence the essential similarity between a diseased condition and its remedy is its symptom-similarity.

A demand having arisen for an official definition of homœopathy, the American Institute of Homœopathy considered the matter, but postponed it for conference with a World's Congress of Homœopathy. In the meanwhile the following is submitted for consideration.*

The subject is too complex to be covered with a simple single definition. There are various ways in which drugs may be similar to diseases; there may be other similarities than those of

---

*J. L. Moffat, *Journal of the American Institute of Homœopathy*, April, 1915.

symptoms between patient and drug, but they can not be relied upon for a cure.

1. Homœopathy is a law* of medicinal therapeutics, cure through symptom-similarity, and is formulated Similia Similibus Curentur—"let likes be treated with likes"—upon the understanding that by "likes" is here meant symptom-similarity.

Hahnemann, an excellent Latin scholar, knew what he meant to say and was indignant at his followers for changing his *curentur* to "curantur."

This Latin phrase formulates the way to select the curative remedy. It expresses the relation, symptom-similarity, between two series of observed facts: (a) the *facts* of disease—all that we can ascertain about the sick patient, and (b) the *facts* of the remedy—all the subjective and objective symptoms that the remedy *has been found to cause* in the healthy body.

2. Homœopathy is a scientific† expression of relationship

*"Law—the uniform occurrence of natural phenomena in the same way or order under the same conditions, so far as human knowledge goes; a formal statement of such uniformity in any given class of cases."—*Standard Dictionary.*

†"Science—the formulation into law of correlations of observed facts."—*Ibid.*

between the science of pathology on the one hand and the science of pharmacology on the other; it is unaffected by advances in knowledge of either of these sciences, except that thereby it may be applied more exactly. Its application is an art.‡

3. Homœopathy is a system of medicine limited, strictly speaking, to medicinal therapeutics, but extending throughout the practice of medicine and surgery wherever and whenever internal medication is applicable. Based upon cure by symptom-similarity and upon individualization of patient, case and remedy, it involves the single remedy, small dose, potentization, provings, verifications, materia medica, pharmacology and a complete organization of societies, colleges, hospitals, etc., books and periodicals peculiar to but not necessarily limited to itself.

President Joseph Ivimey Dowling, in his address to the American Homœopathic Ophthalmological, Otological and Laryngological Society in 1914, defined homœopathy as *a therapeutic drug specialty primarily governed by the*

---

‡James Krauss, M. D., Boston. *Journal of the American Institute of Homœopathy,* March, 1913, p. 936; Aug., 1913, p. 158; Aug., 1914, p. 152.

law of similia similibus curentur, and claimed Hahneman as "the father of all specialists" on account of his thoroughness and because homœopathy was the first specialty upon a scientific basis.

Hahnemann stated plainly that every reasonable physician will first remove removable causes, that local mechanical conditions are to be treated surgically, that in dangerous emergencies antipathic and hygienic palliatives are permissible and useful.

The second tenet of homœopathy (a corollary of the first) is **the single remedy.**

The scientific way to study drug action in disease is to administer but one drug at a time.

The scientific way to learn the action of a drug is to "prove"† it upon the healthy body with due precautions that the symptoms (subjective and objective) observed are properly attributable to the drug. It is well to supplement this with larger, lethal, doses to animals for the study of structural changes. The proper study of the pathogenetic effects of a drug requires many

---

†The best exposition of this, as yet, is the "Reproving of Belladonna." A Test Drug-Proving of the American Homœopathic Ophthalmological, Otological and Laryngological Society. HOWARD P. BELLOWS, M. D., Director and Editor. Published by the Society, Boston. 1906. For sale by Boericke & Tafel.

provings upon numerous people, both males and females, by administering it in varying doses. The same drug affects different parts of the body in different individuals; when a symptom occurs in two or more provers, or is repeated in one prover each time and only when the drug is taken, it carries more weight because it is then certainly more attributable to the drug.

By the **psora miasm** Hahnemann meant a dyscrasia which is typified by that condition of the body in which the sarcoptes scabiei thrives. We all know that one individual is contaminated by the touch of a person or article carrying the itch insect while another escapes as if he or she were repugnant to the insect.

Today Dr. Korndoerfer* offers *lowered immunity from hypothyroidism* as the modern explanation of Hahnemann's much discussed and misunderstood "psora miasm;" he shows the identity of their symptoms.

THE DOSE.

The third tenet of homœopathy is the small dose. Hahnemann found by experience that a

*A Suggested Physiological Basis for Hahnemann's Psora Theory. August Korndoerfer, M. D., Philadelphia. *New England Medical Gazette,* Apr., 1913, p. 170.

patient is particularly sensitive to the remedy when it is homœopathic to his or her condition, that too large a dose will aggravate the disease and may even precipitate death. Hence he diminished his doses, but never to such extremes as did some of his followers. He wrote:* "Pure experiments and observation alone can solve the question of the dose. The doses are to be reduced so far that they will merely produce an almost imperceptible homœopathic aggravation, a slight intensification of the symptoms, immediately after having been taken."

Hahnemann taught the dual action of drugs (which the dominant school has but lately begun to teach). By this is meant, not reaction but, that opposite effects follow the administration of small as compared with large doses, both pathogenetically and therapeutically. The size of the dose must be left to the judgment of the prescriber because it has been found impossible to formulate definite rules for it. Some have said, "Give the smallest (the 'minimum') dose that will cure." The author feels that much harm would have been avoided if this had been put "Do not give so large a dose as to impede the cure or do any harm." Constantine Hering advised that "the more accurately the

*Organon, sections 278, 279, 280.

remedy is selected, the closer and fuller its similarity, the higher should be the potency." The late Professor Henry M. Dearborn, M. D., taught and practiced: "in chronic diseases lower the attenuation, increase the dose, *until some effect be noticed,* for better or worse, then give smaller doses, higher attenuations, or stop the remedy as improvement progresses. This, of course, when one is satisfied that the right remedy has been selected."

The dose will vary according to whether we wish a chemic, mechanic or dynamic effect, also with the drug and the susceptibility of the patient. The patient should be cured "tuto, cito et jucunde." The small dose obviates disturbing the stomach and does not upset the patient or set up a drug condition which is later to be combatted; when a potency acts it is usually more prompt and more thorough than are large doses. Dilution and trituration increase the points of surface contact and thus more than compensate for lessened quantity of drug; possibly, with better knowledge of ionization and radio energy some other explanation may be added to this. The small dose is no longer derided; Sir Almoth E. Wright has put an end to that by demonstrating the opsonic effect of the 1/100,000th of a milligram of tuberculin. Burrett and others in this country have shown by laboratory experimentation that homœopathic remedies excite the development or the activity of the natural immunizing elements in the body, such as raising the opsonic index. Is not this a twentieth century way of saying, with Hahnemann, that homœopathy follows nature in its method of cure?

Some weight should be given to the fact that many homœopathic physicians have come to rely on "high potencies" because they have had better success with them than when practicing allopathically, empirically or with tinctures and massive doses.

While the homœopathic remedy is usually administered by mouth and rarely by olfaction, it may be applied locally and at times can best be given hypodermatically.

Broadly speaking, the homœopathic prescription is usually based upon the drug's secondary symptoms, while the dominant school administers a remedy for its primary effect. Belladonna, in large dose, is mydriatic; mydriasis, when not due to atropin or belladonna, is one of the important indications for the administration, homœopathically, of belladonna—the accompanying condition is best met with a smaller dose than one which would dilate the pupil if administered internally.

A fundamental principle of homœopathic practice is **individualization**—individualization of patient, of case and of remedy. It is the patient who is sick and is to be restored to health, not the disease that is to be combatted and cured.

Diagnosis is essential for intelligent therapeutics, but the symptoms of most importance in making the diagnosis are not the most important ones in selecting the remedy. This is because the generic symptoms, while classifying disease, are not particular enough to characterize the individual case of illness. So-called physiological prescribing points out a class of remedies but fails to indicate which one is to be chosen. For this, reliance must be placed upon the peculiar symptoms—those peculiar to the case; they may be unexplainable and apparently trifling. Among these are the modalities—conditions of aggravation and amelioration, of time, location, etc. Mental symptoms are very important for the selection of the remedy and, as a class, subjective are more valuable than objective symptoms when prescribing.

There are varying degrees of similarity; the more complete the similarity the more satisfactory will be the cure. While the most brilliant homœopathic cures have been constitutional, the principle is often applicable in apparently local troubles with but few symptoms. A remedy is often given, with gratifying result, upon only three or four "characteristic" symptoms; it often relieves one phase of a disease which may be incurable or which may require a succession of remedies or other treatment for its cure.

Years ago an intelligent patient, blind from cerebral tumor, suffered intensely with sudden sharp agonizing neuralgic pains in the head—requiring morphine. The after-effects of this were such that she would beg me (until the next attack) to give her anything but that drug.

One day prunus spinosa (if I remember aright) seemed called for by the bursting character of the pain. A single dose—pellets medicated with the tincture—stopped the pain, not only for a longer while, but much more promptly and completely than did morphine. But alas, that lost its effect and the case pursued the usual sad course.

VERIFICATIONS.

Verifications—cures of symptoms under the homœopathic law—form an essential part of homœopathic literature, provided they are properly reported.

Every clinical report should be so clear and full that the reader or hearer will agree with the reporter in the diagnosis and will concede that the cure or relief claimed is properly

attributable to the remedy (or treatment, whatever that was) and to nothing else. Care should be taken to mention all adjuvant treatment and other change in environment, the duration of the symptoms or disease and also the promptness, completeness and permanence of relief. Its value will be increased by indicating the symptoms which led to the selection of the remedy. The following may be considered

A MODEL CLINICAL REPORT.

"**Rhus toxicodendron for panophthalmitis following cataract extraction.*** James L., age 67, mature cataract of right eye. A preliminary iridectomy had been made three weeks previously, healing nicely with no complications. The extraction was made under usual precautions with no untoward results.

"The second day after the operation on dressing the wound noticed the lids decidedly red, swollen and puffy. Examination of the eye showed profuse lacrimation with an edematous chemosis. The wound had been closed and anterior chamber re-established, but there was noticed a slight haziness along the line of the incision. Atropin 1 per cent. was instilled, the dressing re-applied, an ice bag ordered laid on the side of the eye and rhus toxicodendron 3x was given.

---

*Arthur B. Norton, M. D., New York. Trans. American Homœopathic Ophthalmological, Otological and Laryngological Society, 1904, p. 185.

"The following day the eye looked very much worse. The swelling of the lids had increased and was somewhat harder. The chemosis was decidedly worse, denser and less edematous. The haziness of the cornea at the line of incision had extended and there was commencing hypopion. There was quite severe pain in the eye and head, much worse during the night. The eye looked bad; panophthalmitis was diagnosed and an unfavorable prognosis given. The same treatment was continued, except that the rhus was given five drops of tincture in one-half glass of water, a teaspoonful every hour.

"I certainly thought the eye was lost, as the change for the worse in 24 hours with the patient taking rhus all the time was decided. As the remedy seemed indicated, and as it always has been my sheet-anchor in panophthalmitis, it was continued but given lower. The next day no change for the worse; as far as I could judge the eye had held its own, and the remedy was continued.

"Two days later there was without doubt marked improvement: the aqueous was clearer, the chemosis not so great, and the pain was less. From this time on the case steadily progressed, the chemosis disappearing, the cornea clearing, and the eye went on to perfect recovery with no loss of vision.

"I believe that the change to the tincture saved this eye; it was steadily progressing under the potency and began to respond only after the tincture was used. I have noticed this same action since, and now always use rhus tox. in the tincture in water for panophthalmitis."

The curative remedy for a given case of iritis will be found not by depending upon the diagnostic symptoms—belladonna, bryonia, mercurius, spigelia and each of more than twenty other drugs may cause these—but that one must be chosen which has the characteristic, individualizing symptoms presented by the individual case; sometimes it may be a remedy that has never been known to cause or cure iritis and the symptoms pointing out the remedy will probably be elsewhere than in the eye.

If the patient is rheumatic, irritable, constipated, aggravated by heat and motion, is worse in the morning, has soreness in, around and behind the eyeball, with sticking pains in the eyes—bryonia will cure, whether the pathological condition be muscular or an iritis.

But the mercurius patient presents an entirely different picture: he is worse at night after going to bed and in damp weather, the eyes are particularly sensitive to the fire-light and heat, light of the gas, etc., he has night sweats, nocturnal pains in different parts of the body, metallic taste in the mouth, the tongue is flabby and indented, there may be a diarrhœa—all or most of these symptoms in addition to those of iritis proper.

Spigelia, usually classed as a neuralgia remedy, has repeatedly made brilliant cures of iritis when indicated by the totality of symptoms, characterized usually by neuralgic pains radiating from the eye through the temple, face and head.

It makes, sometimes, just the difference between success and failure—the quality of the medicine used. Strange to say, a shockingly large number of doctors buy the cheapest—not the best—medicines that they can, or dare. They risk the patient's life or health upon the effect of an inferior preparation. Cheap medicines are necessarily inferior. Tinctures prepared by a reliable homœopathic pharmacy are acknowledgedly better than any others, and so with the triturations. Surely it would be unfair to condemn homœopathy because of failure with medicine which was not made according to the directions or with the care of the homœopathic pharmacopœia!

Even after the lapse of a hundred years our provings are still incomplete; they should be brought up to date with the use of modern instruments of precision. This will be done eventually, but the amount of work involved will be enormous.

The best books for studying the homœopathic materia medica are: Farrington's Lectures on Materia Medica, Kent's Lectures on Materia Medica, and Hughes' Pharmacodynamics. Some object to the last named that it teaches organotherapy and pathological drug action rather than strict homœopathy. The classical work on homœopathy applied to ophthalmology has been Norton's "Ophthalmic Diseases and Therapeutics."*

Homœopathy is not organotherapy, yet some remedies do undoubtedly manifest a selective action upon certain organs or tissues: *e. g.*, belladonna, duboisia, gelsemium, mercurius corrosivus, phosphorus, each may cause congestion or inflammation of the fundus even when introduced into the stomach or some other part of the system remote from the eye.

It is impossible to memorize the homœopathic materia medica, nor all the symptoms of any one of our leading remedies; recourse must be had to repertories followed by consultation of the materia medica. It is because of this difficulty that the majority of oculists who believe in homœopathy feel that they do not have time—from the stress of work and demands of other phases of medical study—to apply it properly in their daily practice. As a matter of fact very many so-called homœopathic prescriptions are but empirical; *e. g.*, bryonia given "for iritis" on the recommendation of a fellow practitioner might happen to be a stumbled upon, empirical, cure so far as

*Third edition, 1902. Boericke & Tafel, Philadelphia.

the prescriber is concerned, but (unless due to other treatment or the vis medicatrix naturæ) the symptoms, either unnoted or unappreciated, would show the cure to be really although unwittingly a homœopathic one. Needless to say it would be more scientific, more certain, and the doctor would have learned more if it had been given because of its symptom-similarity. It is a well established fact that the oculist finds himself well repaid for conscientious study of the homœopathic materia medica.

A prescription is homœopathic only when the medicine is selected, and because it is selected, upon the homœopathic principle, whether consciously or unconsciously.

The official definition of the homœopathic physician is: "One who *adds to* his knowledge of medicine a special knowledge of homœopathic therapeutics and observes the law of Similia. All that pertains to the great field of medicine is his by tradition, by inheritance, by right."

The homœopathic practitioner is a specialist, some are exclusivists.

CHAPTER III.

MATERIA MEDICA.

ACETIC ACID—Acet. ac.

$HC_2H_3O_2$.

Objective.—Eyes sunken, surrounded by dark circles. Lacrimation.

Clinical.—Has proved of value in croupous conjunctivitis (not diphtheritic) with closely adherent, tough, dense, yellowish-white false membrane which leaves no scars and does not penetrate deeply. The lids are red, edematous, the upper hangs down over the lower, and at no time are they rigidly infiltrated.

ACONITUM NAPELLUS—Acon.

Wolf's Bane. Monk's Hood.

Objective.—Lids red, swollen, hard, especially the upper; < morning. Edges sore, inflamed. Chemosis. *Conjunctiva intensely hyperæmic and edematous,* mostly toward the inner canthus. Lacrimation slight, if any.

Subjective.—Eyes *burn, feel dry, sensitive to air.* Much *aching* and *heat.* Intense burning shooting pains. Pressure upon upper lids, as if the ball were pushed into the orbit, causing a bruised pain in the eye. Itching; smarting; < evening. The ball, especially the upper half, sensitive if moved; < looking down or turning the eyes; the ball feels enlarged, as if protruding, making the lids tense; feels as if it would be forced out of the orbit, > stooping. Eyes feel swollen. *Feel as if sand were in them.* Photophobia.

Vision.—As through a veil; difficult to distinguish faces. Sparks before the eyes; flickering.

Characteristics.—The aconite patient is characterized by *great anxiety, fear, restlessness and thirst. First stage of inflammation, or trauma of cornea, conjunctiva, sclera, lids.*

Clinical.—*The routine remedy with foreign bodies, wounds, operations, and for neuralgia from exposure to a cold dry wind.*

AGARICUS MUSCARIUS—Agar.

Bug Agaric. Amanita mushroom.

Objective.—*Twitches in or of the lids;* contracted palpebral fissure without swelling. Very little appearance of inflammation. Twitching of (in) the ball, often painful while reading, < left. Myosis.

Subjective.—Biting, itching, jerking in the lids

and brow. Aching and pressure in the ball, it is sensitive to touch; *burning and itching;* stitches. Eyes feel very weak.

Vision.—Dim, as in a mist, with *flickering.* Reading difficult, as *type seems to move, to swim.* Yellow spots when looking at white. "Vibrating spectra." Muscæ volitantes. Short sighted. *All objects look blue.*

Clinical.—Particularly useful in asthenopia from prolonged strain; weakness, fibrillar spasms.

ALLIUM CEPA—See Cepa.

ALOE SOCOTRINA—Aloe.

Aloes.

Subjective.—Heaviness, with frontal ache and nausea. During frontal headache has to make eyes small, which relieves. *Pain deep in orbits, as if in muscles, < right.*

Vision.—Yellow rings move before the eyes.

Characteristics.—Heaviness, of eyes, head, back, abdomen.

Clinical.—Reflex from or accompanying uterine or bowel congestion or inflammation.

ALUMINA—Alum.

Aluminum hydrate. $Al(OH)_3$.

Objective.—Upper lids seem to hang as if paralyzed, < left. Lids twitch, < right upper; agglutinated on waking. Squinting. Conjunctiva red, inflamed, < right, < evening.

Subjective.—Burning and dryness; in the evening; < on looking up. Pressure, heaviness, difficult to open the eyes. Itching in the canthi. Photophobia.

Vision.—Dim, as through a fog, or as if hairs or feathers were before the eyes; with sensation as though the lids would adhere at the corners. < evening.

Characteristics.—Paralysis of motor nerves. Is one of the leading remedies for locomotor ataxia.

Clinical.—Chronic granular or follicular conjunctivitis with dryness and loss of power in the lids.

ANTIMONIUM CRUDUM—Ant. cr.

Antimonium sulphid. Sb_2S_3.

Objective.—Lids red, inflamed, excoriated; agglutinated. Outer canthi sore.

Subjective.—Itching. Soreness. Photophobia.

Characteristics.—Acts on mucous membranes, depression and excessive secretion. Cross, "devilish" children, and older persons. Tongue coated very thick white. Alternate constipation and diarrhœa.

Clinical.—Blepharitis, and scrofulous ophthalmia, with pustules on face, or cornea, or conjunctiva.

ANTIMONIUM TARTARICUM—Ant. t.

Potassium Antimonyl Tartrate.

Tartar emetic. $2K(SbO)C_4H_4O_6+H_2O$.

Objective.—Eyes squint. Eyes fixed and turned upward. Surrounded by blue rings and lying deep in their sockets. Swollen. *Bloodshot.* Mydriasis. Sclera yellow.

Subjective.—Pressure on eyes. Burning in evening. Burning in right inner canthus, with biting and redness of conjunctiva. Electric stitches in inner canthi, with pressure in eyes. Sudden tensive pain in upper part of right ball. Bruised feeling in eyeball, $<$ touch. Eyes *weak.* *Inclined to press lids tightly together.* Lids difficult to move.

Vision.—*Flickering;* $<$ *rising from seat, with vision as through a veil* and vertigo. Sparks. Vanishing of vision.

Characteristics.—Profound depression, of heart, pulse and temperature. Rapid tissue waste. Nausea, vomiting. Children fretful. *Loose cough with rattling in the chest but comparatively little expectoration.*

Clinical.—*Phlyctenular ophthalmia. Herpes of the conjunctiva. Photophobia.*

APIS MELLIFICA—Apis.

The Honey Bee.

The tincture is made from the live honey bee, and is but little stronger than the 3x trituration of Apium virus, which is made by extracting and triturating the poison sac.

Objective.—*Lids much swollen, pale red edema.* Upper one hangs like a sac. Conjunctiva inflamed, *edematous,* with dark red veins. *Lacrimation;* hot. Agglutination.

Subjective.—*Itching. Stinging, sharp piercing pains in and about the eyes.* Burning, stinging which causes lacrimation. Soreness and smarting in the eyes, lid edges and canthi. Fullness. Photophobia. Eyes pain and are easily fatigued. Sensation of a foreign body.

Vision.—Obscured, difficult, with a whirling. Pain on using eyes.

Characteristics.—*Thirstless, even with fever, and drowsiness. Edema. Dropsy;* skin waxy white.

Clinical.—Erysipelas. Albuminuric retinitis. Useful in various forms of keratitis. Purulent edema. As a rule, temporary > from applying cold water. An extremely valuable remedy in inflammatory affections of the eyes *always characterized by serous exudation, edema and sudden piercing pains.*

ARGENTUM NITRICUM—Arg. n.

Nitrate of Silver. $AgNO_3$.

Objective.—Eyes closed by swollen inflamed lids. Ocular and palpebral conjunctiva and *caruncle intensely swollen, red and inflamed.* Clusters of intensely red bloodvessels from inner canthus to cornea; discharge *profuse, bland, mucopurulent or of thick yellow pus.* Cornea opaque, may be covered with conjunctival folds. Lacrimation.

Subjective.—*Photophobia and pain are intense.* Heaviness over the eyes, which open with difficulty. Boring above left eye. Infraorbital neuralgia. Burning, biting, itching in the eyes, particularly in the canthi. Heat and pain in the ball, upon motion and touch; aching pain deep in the eye, early in the morning. All symptoms < by heat.

Vision.—*Gray spots and serpent-like bodies move before the eyes.* Sudden vanishing of sight from inability to maintain the focus.

Characteristics.—*Craving for, and aggravation from, sweets. Much wind in stomach, also in the bowels.* Typically, the argentum nitricum patient is dark, thin, easily angered, often the more one tries to do for him the more disagreeable he becomes; he is apprehensive, fearful. *He is hurried, walks fast, does not undertake a thing* *lest he should not succeed. Very virulent ophthalmia, the attack reaching in a few hours a condition that the pulsatilla patient would take days to achieve.* The discharge in both patients is thick and bland, and both are *aggravated by heat;* with argentum the heat from a stove is particularly unbearable.

Clinical.—*The* great remedy, internally as well as locally, for *ophthalmia neonatorum and gonorrhœal ophthalmia.* A valuable remedy for asthenopia from masturbation. Early stages of acute granular conjunctivitis: the eyes may feel dry and burn when there is no real dryness; the discharge may be only a few flakes of mucus; *the palpebral conjunctiva looks like velvet.*

ARNICA MONTANA—Arn.

Leopard's Bane.

Undiluted tincture locally to the eye is sometimes irritating; this has been attributed to an insect in the flower.

Objective.—Eyes inflamed. Slight lacrimation.

Subjective.—Margins of upper lids painful on motion, as if they were dry and a little sore. Feeling of heaviness in the eyes; some burning, itching, photophobia. Cramp-like tearing or pressure in left brow.

Characteristics.—A *bruised sore feeling,* and *weariness.*

Clinical.—Arnica is the great remedy, locally and internally, to promote *absorption of extravasated blood in the eye or any part of the body. It is the remedy for bruises.* The tincture acts better locally when diluted to, say, 2 per cent. (a dram to 6 ounces of water).

ARSENICUM ALBUM—Ars.

White Arsenic. Arsenious Acid. A. Oxid. As_2O_3.

Objective.—*Lids edematous, swollen* (usually noninflammatory and painless). Edematous lids firmly closed and look as if distended with air. Conjunctiva, palpebral or ocular, inflamed. *Burning, acrid lacrimation making the lids and cheeks red and sore.*

Subjective.—*Severe burning, or burning pain,* in the eyes, *in the lid edges.* Eyes feel dry as if rubbed by the lids. Feeling of sand, obliging him to rub the eyes, in the evening. Eyes hot, with burning sore pain in the balls and a feeling as though they had no room in the orbit. Pulsative throbbing in the eyes and with every pulsation a stitch; after midnight. Suborbital pain, left, with pricking as with needles. Ciliary neuralgia, *fine burning pains. Photophobia.*

Characteristics.—*Great restlessness and anx-*

iety, with weakness, prostration, and thirst for very frequent small drinks. < after midnight, 1 a. m. Burning pains. Emaciation. Generally > by warm applications. *Anguish. Despair. Dread of death.*

Clinical.—Puffy below the eyes. *Corneal ulcer.* Scrofulous ophthalmia. Chronic trachoma. Keratitis. Iritis. Disseminate choroiditis. Hyperthyroidism.

ASAFETIDA—Asa.

Subjective.—*Severe boring (bone) pains above the brows; > by pressure.* Troublesome dryness. Periodic burning in the eyes and pressing together of the lids, as if overcome by sleep. Burning pain in the ball from within outward. Throbbing pain at night, > by pressure.

Characteristics.—The action is most marked on the nervous system; has been valuable in mercurial and scrofulous affections of the bones and skin. The pains, > by rest and by pressure (reverse of aurum), are usually throbbing, beating, boring or burning in, over or around the eye; often intermittent; they extend from within outward.

Clinical.—Ciliary neuralgia. Syphilitic iritis. Hysterical persons.

AURUM METALLICUM—Aur. met.

Gold. Au.

Objective.—*Eyes protrude. Constant lacrimation. Morning agglutination.*

Subjective.—*Feeling of sand. Heat; when looking; as if blood pressed upon optic nerve. Feeling of weakness and pressure. Pressive pain in right eye, from above downward or inward, < during motion. Burning in lids, in inner canthi, with stitching, drawing and itching.*

Vision.—Tension making vision difficult; < fixing eyes, > closing them, with diminished vision. *Vision double, and one object is seen mixed with another, with tension in eyes. Upper hemianopsia: upper half of the field invisible. Vision indistinct, as through a black veil.*

Characteristics.—*Melancholy.* Despair. Self condemnation. Suicidal. Mental anguish, with precordial distress. Hyperemia, fullness of the bloodvessels.

AURUM MURIATICUM—Aur. mur.

Chlorid of Gold. Auric chlorid. $AuCl_3$.

As is the case with some other metallic remedies, the symptoms of the metal and its chlorid are so much the same that some give the metal when prescribing a high attenuation and its salt in the larger dose or lower potency.

Objective.—Redness and swelling of the lids. Redness of the sclera. Eyes very red and angry looking. Morning agglutination. Constant lacrimation.

Subjective.—Photophobia. Burning, stitching, drawing and itching in lids and inner canthus. Heat in the eye when looking. Feeling of sand. Pressive pain (right) above downward, also *from without inward, < touch or pressure.* Bones around the eye feel bruised. Pains boring and < at night.

Vision.—*Hemianopsia, upper half of the field seems covered with a black body. Diplopia. Sees things double, mixed up,* with violent tension in the eyes. Vision indistinct, as through a veil.

Characteristics.—*The aurum patient is mentally depressed, very blue,* irritable, sensitive to noise, usually with swollen cervical glands. Pains seem to be deep in the bone. Eye sensitive to touch.

Clinical.—Aurum is one of the principal syphilitico-mercurial remedies. For *trachoma with,* or without, *pannus* there is no remedy more useful. Usually < morning and > by application of cold water. *Interstitial,* ulcerous or vascular *keratitis;* iritis and kerato-iritis, particularly after abuse of mercury, or if syphilitic or due to hereditary syphilis. Aurum is almost specific for *exudative chorio-retinitis and exudations into the vitreous.*

BADIAGA—Bad.

Fresh Water Sponge.

Objective.—Bluish purple margins of lids. Scrofulous inflammation with hardening of the Meibomian glands.

Subjective.—Headache extending into the eyeballs. Slight aching pains in posterior portion of both eyeballs and in the temples, with headache, from 2 p. m. till 7 a. m. Left eyeball quite sore, even when closing it tightly. Severe intermittent pain in the back of the eyeball.

Characteristics.—Lymphatic glands large and hard.

Clinical.—Has been useful in exophthalmic goiter, scrofulous ophthalmia, ocular neuralgia.

BARYTA CARBONICA—Bar. c.

Barium carbonate. $BaCO_3$.

Objective.—Red conjunctiva, swollen lids and dryness of the eyes.

Subjective.—Photophobia. Eyes itch.

Vision.—Light dazzles and hurts the eyes, with fiery spots in the dark. "Gauze" before the eyes in the morning and after a meal. Weakness of sight.

Characteristics.—This remedy affects nutrition profoundly: causes symptoms of malnutrition and consequent degenerative tissue changes; irritates and depresses the cerebral and ganglionic nervous systems to a picture of mental and physical decay; is particularly useful for glandular affections of the throat and neck.

Clinical.—It has checked the advance of cataract.

BELLADONNA—Bell.

Deadly Nightshade.

Objective.—*Pupil dilated; sluggish, or immobile dilated. Eyes red;* lid margins congested; inflamed. Conjunctiva congested; inflamed. Lids droop; twitch; are puffy. On lids: stye, pimples, pustule. Eyes dry, no tears (or mucus and tears increased). Increased ocular tension. *Fundus congested; discs congested, edge not distinct; retina slightly hazy.* Eyes protruding, *bright,* staring, swollen with *red face;* in constant motion.

Muscle balance: at distance, esophoria preponderatingly increased; near, esophoria increased.

Subjective.—*Photophobia.* Eyes feel *dry, stiff, < motion; burning heat.* Pain, pressive, in or about or back of eyes; sharp, neuralgic aching, throbbing; *comes on and passes off quickly.* Eyes smart; itch; feel tired, weak, heavy; tender to pressure.

Vision.—*Dim, blurred;* acuity decreased. Accommodative power impaired; near point for diamond type removed; vision best or only at distance. Letters blur while reading; must hold the paper farther away; could read only while the paper was kept in motion. Everything turned black; blindness. > wiping the eyes; > covering either eye; near objects look smaller (when one eye is covered). Consensual action of pupils diminished. Diplopia, laterally also vertically; vertical strokes of letters looked double; when writing a line looked doubled, the upper black and the lower red. *Erythropsia; everything he looks at seems red. Halo around the (candle) light,* partly colored, red predominating; at times the light seems broken into rays. *Photopsies, flashes, bright sparks.* Flickering. Black spots and stripes before the eyes, when walking in open air, rapidly appearing and disappearing. Objects passing before the eyes have an undulating motion. Objects appear crooked.

Characteristics.—Belladonna is particularly useful, with the above symptoms, in patients with *high blood pressure;* sthenic congestion and inflammation. *Mydriasis. Flushed face.* Pains increase and decrease suddenly.

Clinical.—Its use in inflammatory ocular diseases is more limited than is generally supposed. It has been most valuable in diseases of the fundus: hyperæmia, inflammation of the choroid, especially disseminate choroiditis; retinal hyperesthesia, due to refraction or reflex irritation; *hyperæmia* of the optic nerve and retina, either acute or chronic, particularly if dependent upon cerebral congestion. Is one of the chief remedies in *optic neuritis, neuro-retinitis, retinitis, retinitis hæmorrhagica,* has relieved iritis, idiopathic and post-operative plastic, early stages (dryness) of catarrhal conjunctivitis, erythema and erysipelatous inflammation of the lids, the severe pains of *glaucoma* (do not give material doses here lest the condition be made worse), mydriasis from nervous headache, infraorbital neuralgia with red face and hot hands, amblyopia, amaurosis, paretic accommodative asthenopia, convulsive movements of the eyeball, and spasmodic strabismus, particularly with brain affections.

BORAX—Borax.

Sodium pyroborate. $Na_2B_4O_7+10H_2O$.

Objective.—Lashes turn into and inflame the eye, especially at outer canthus where the lid margins are very sore. Lashes irregular. Nocturnal agglutination. Left inner canthus inflamed.

Vision.—Bright waves, moving now from right to left, now from above downward, mornings when writing.

Characteristics.—*Dread of downward motion.*

Clinical.—Marginal blepharitis. Madarosis. Entropion. Trichiasis.

BOTHROPS LANCEOLATUS—Both.

Yellow Viper.

Vision.—Hemeralopia, day-blindness; can scarcely see her way after sunrise. Aphasia.

BRYONIA ALBA—Bry.

White Bryony.

Objective.—Puffiness of right upper lid; morning agglutination. Conjunctiva dark red and swollen. Lacrimation.

Subjective.—*Photophobia.* Pressive pain above left eye. Pressure, inward, over left orbit into brain which changes to a pressure on the eyeball from above downward. Pain deep in right orbit, < pressure on the ball. Drawing and heaviness in left upper lid. *Very sensitive pressing intermitting pain* in left ball, *especially violent on moving the eye,* with a feeling as if the eye became smaller and retracted in the orbit.

Severe burning, with lacrimation, in right eye. *Eye very sore, < moving it.*

Vision.—Dim. Every object appears covered with rainbow colors; *appearance of all the colors of the rainbow.* Letters run together, on near vision.

Characteristics.—< motion, < heat. Bryonia's great sphere of usefulness is in diseases of the uveal tract in *rheumatic subjects, aggravated by motion, and by warmth, and for serous inflammations with these aggravations.*

Clinical.—It is the first remedy thought of in *rheumatic iritis—sharp shooting pains through the eye into the head, < motion, > pressure;* or steady aching in posterior part of the eye extending through to the occiput, < night and motion. It has checked *glaucoma* and proven valuable in *serous iridochoroiditis and in ciliary neuralgia.*

CALCAREA CARBONICA—Calc. c.

Calcium carbonate. $CaCO_3$.

Hahnemann prepared this from the inside of oyster shells, hence it is sometimes called calcarea ostrearum. When calcarea alone is mentioned the carbonate is meant.

Objective.—Swelling and redness of the lids,

with nightly agglutination. Lids hard, swollen, with dry scales. Upper lids twitch. Redness of the eyes. Eyes full of mucus. Acrid lacrimation.

Subjective.—Pain like a foreign body in the eye, like sand. Sticking pains in the eyes. Itching, burning and stitches, particularly in the lid margins and inner canthi. Pressure and itching in the eyes, $>$ evenings.

Vision.—Dim, after getting the head cold. Hemianopsia, only one side of objects visible, with dilated pupils. Halo around the light. Flickering, sparks, black spots.

Characteristics.—Calcarea is the typical remedy for malnutrition in scrofulous, tubercular, rachitic subjects with indurated glands, particularly if the trouble is caused by getting wet and cold or *by working in water. Pot-bellied children who sweat profusely about the head. Fat blondes with enlarged indurated glands. Leucophlegmatic temperament.* The general condition is more important for the prescription than are the symptoms.

Clinical.—*Scrofulous ophthalmia;* blepharitis; acute conjunctivitis either phlyctenular, pustular or purulent; keratitis—ulcerative, phlyctenular, pustular; corneal opacities; trachoma; pterygium; asthenopia.

CALCAREA HYPOPHOSPHOROSA—

Calc. hy.

Calcium hypophosphite. $Ca(PO_2)_2$.

Clinical.—This has proved to be a remedy of the first importance for *severe abscess or ulceration of the cornea,* even sloughing or crescentic, when the vitality is too low to resist the disease. Sometimes there is complicating iritis or hypopion.

CALCAREA IODATA—Calc. iod.

Calcium iodid. CaI_2.

Clinical.—This salt is to be thought of in *acute exacerbations of chronic "calcarea" diseases;* the patient is often thin with dark hair instead of blonde and fat. The *ulcers and pustules,* particularly of the cornea, have intense pain, photophobia, lacrimation, lid spasms, and often acute inflammation of tonsils or other glands. The patient is very susceptible to cold, the eye inflammation is $<$ by the least cold. Chronic blepharitis; erysipelatous or scrofulous inflammation of the lids. Conical cornea and staphyloma have been checked.

CALCAREA PHOSPHORICA—Calc. phos.

Calcium orthophosphate. $Ca_3(PO_4)_2$.

Objective.—Eyes red. Injected streaks from canthi to cornea.*

Subjective.—Photophobia, particularly in candle or gas light; can not read. Sensation of something in the eye, felt if it is mentioned.

Vision.—Photopsia. Glittering circles of light before the eyes.

Clinical.—Valuable for parenchymatous keratitis in patients of a scrofulous diathesis, and in checking the progress of cataract.

CALCAREA SULPHURICA—Calc. s.

Calcium sulphate. $CaSO_4$.

Objective.—*Very profuse, thick, very yellow,* lumpy, *pus* or mucus. Hypopion. Haziness or ulceration of cornea; phlyctenular or pustular keratitis with enlarged cervical glands.

Vision.—Hemianopsia.

Clinical.—A great remedy for suppuration after the above described pus has obtained a vent.

---

*Suggestive of a nasal origin or complication if obstinate.

CANNABIS SATIVA—Can. sat.

Hemp.

Clinical.—Parenchymatous keratitis, cornea covered with bloodvessels; profuse lacrimation, intense photophobia. Acts best low.

CARBO VEGETABILIS—C. veg.

Vegetable Charcoal from birch or beech.

Subjective.—Heavy weight seems to rest on the eyes, must make effort to distinguish letters when reading. Eyes weak and ache from overwork. Eyes burn. Itching in the lid margins and about the eyes. The eye muscles pain when looking up.

Vision.—He became shortsighted after exerting the eye for awhile. Muscæ volitantes.

Characteristics.—A very valuable remedy when the blood is devitalized and the nervous system exhausted—as in scorbutus; purpura, persistent passive dark venous hæmorrhages. Collapse: body cold, skin bluish, cold sweat on limbs, breath cool, pulse thready, intermittent—it has plucked many such patients from the jaws of death, but was then given in the 30th or 200th attenuation. Very characteristic symptoms are: *violent, almost constant, eructations. Sour stomach; burning. Abdomen full of flatus, to bursting, with colic.*

< from the least food, > passing gas up or down. Burning pains in various places. *Patient wants to be fanned.*

Clinical.—Norton thinks this should be used in eye diseases. It has proved beneficial in asthenopia, and he suggests its use for progressive myopia with posterior staphyloma.

CAUSTICUM—Caust.

"Tinctura acris sine kali."

A weak preparation of potassium hydrate of uncertain strength, introduced by Hahnemann; it should therefore be made strictly according to his directions.

Objective.—Pupils dilated. Visible twitches in lids, and left eyebrow. Eyes inflamed, lids red. Lacrimation, < in open air.

Subjective.—*Pressure as if sand were in the eyes. Dryness, photophobia, burning and stinging* with the inflammation. Pressive pain in eyes, < by touch. Itching, specially in lids, disappears on rubbing. Itching in lower lid and its inner surface, with burning as soon as he touches or moves the eye. Biting and pressure in the eyes, which seem heavy, with redness of the lid. *Inclination to close the eyes,* they close involuntarily. *Sensation of heaviness in upper lid* as if he could not raise it easily, or as if it were stuck to the lower lid and could not easily be loosened. Opening the lids is difficult. Burning and itching in the inner canthi. Photophobia with constant necessity to wink.

Vision.—Flickering, like swarms of insects. Photopsies, sparks, on winking, even on a bright day. *Vision indistinct, dim,* as though a thick cloud or veil were before the eyes; transient obscuration on blowing the nose. Diplopia, paretic, < turning the eyes to the right.

Characteristics.—The patient, while sensitive to cold and cold drinks, is better in rainy weather.

Clinical.—This remedy has been credited with curing warts on the lid and brow, blepharitis > in fresh air and simple acute conjunctivitis. Many cases of cataract have been arrested and even improved. But the main sphere of action is *peripheral paralysis* of the muscles—levator palpebræ superioris, orbicularis, external rectus and ciliary muscle—in fact, any muscle if due to exposure to cold dry wind or if following diphtheria. Causticum is the principal remedy for *ptosis* and paretic *aphonia* (postdiphtheritic); it is not recommended in syphilitic cases.

CEDRON—Ced.

Simaba Cedron. Rattlesnake Bean.

Subjective.—*Severe shooting pain over the left eye.* Pain across the eyes from temple to temple. Severe pain in the eyeball, radiating pains all around the eye, shooting into nose. Scalding lacrimation.

Characteristics.—*Supraorbital neuralgia, periodic;* more often over the left eye, may follow the branches of the supraorbital nerve into the head. The pains, usually sharp, may come and go suddenly; < may be evening or lying down. *Clock-like regularity.*

Clinical.—Particularly useful in tropical countries, or for troubles in or from a damp warm marshy locality. Iritis, choroiditis, neuralgia as above.

CEPA—Cepa.

Allium Cepa. The Common Red Onion.

Objective.—*Lacrimation with coryza. Lacrimation, < left, with redness of the eyeball; not excoriating. < in evening, in warm room.* Redness, < left.

Subjective.—*Biting,* as if there were smoke under the upper lids, < night. *Pain as if the eyes hung loose posteriorly on a string,* could be bored into with the fingers and torn out. Burning and smarting in the eyes as from smoke, wants to rub them. Stitches, left, in the morning. > open air. Sensation as if something were under the lid. *Sensitive to light.*

Vision.—Dazzling at distance and dim near by. Flickering and blindness.

Clinical.—This remedy is unrivaled for *acute fluent coryza, catarrhal conjunctivitis, profuse burning and smarting but not acrid coryza, with profuse watery very acrid discharge from the nose and usually sneezing. Ciliary neuralgia after cataract extraction* (give five drop doses of the tincture.—Liebold). This dosage relieved most promptly a case of iridochoroiditis.

CHAMOMILLA—Cham.

Chamomile.

Objective.—Lids swollen in morning, agglutinated. Purulent mucus. Conjunctiva swollen and dark red. Lacrimation.

Subjective.—Intense photophobia. Heat, burning in the eyes. Stitches in the orbital region and soreness in the canthi. Pressure in the orbital region; in the eyes; sensation in the eyeball as if compressed from all sides.

Vision.—Momentarily obscured with the last mentioned symptom.

Characteristics.—The keynote of chamomilla is *excessive sensitiveness,* the nerves seem bare, on edge. *Pains, sensations are unbearable; hence irritable, cross, peevish.*

Clinical.—Has been used, internally and locally, for conjunctivitis, and scrofulous ophthalmia, relieving suffering although some other remedy will be necessary for the cure.

CHELIDONIUM MAJUS—Chel.

Celandine.

Objective.—*Sclera looks dirty yellow.* Lids twitch; margins red and swollen. Lacrimation.

Subjective.—*Neuralgic pain above right eye, >evening,* when reading by artificial light; *aching or pain in balls when looking up* or moving the eyes. Sharp piercing stitching pains; tearing pain in and about the eyes. Left eye, pressive pain which seems to press down the upper lid.

Vision.—Dimness. Blackness with sensation of fainting. A blinding spot, lacrimation on looking at it.

Characteristics.—Chelidonium acts principally on the liver: congestion, inflammation, jaundice; its characteristic symptom is *constant pain in or under the lower corner of the right scapula.*

CHINA—China.

Cinchona Officinalis. C. Calisaya. Peruvian Bark.

Objective.—Whites of eyes yellow. Lacrimation.

Subjective.—*Pressure in eyes.* Photophobia. Motion of eyes painful with sensation of mechanical hindrance. Crawling pain in eyes and inner surface of lids, with lacrimation. Neuralgic pains in or about the eyes.

Vision.—Dim.

Characteristics.—Anæmia. Nervous erythism with debility. Vertigo.

Clinical.—Nyctalopia from anæmia. Not often called for in ocular therapeutics except when for consequences of *loss of vital fluids,* or of malaria. Neuralgia. Leucocythæmia. There may be periodicity. Loss of tone.

CHININUM ARSENICOSUM—Chin. ars.

Quinine Arsenite. $(C_{20}H_{24}N_2O_2)_3H_3As_2O_3 3H_2O$.

Clinical.—Has proved useful in scrofulous ophthalmia, < after midnight, till 3 a. m.; keratitis; corneal ulcer, gushing hot tears, intense photophobia, spasm of orbicularis; flickering before left eye with pain and lacrimation, in hemicrania. Weariness. General prostration.

CHININUM MURIATICUM—Chin. m.

Quinine muriate. Q. hydrochlorate.

$C_{20}H_{24}N_2O_2HCl.2H_2O$.

Clinical.—This, in appreciable doses, has controlled *severe neuralgic pains occurring in iritis; if the pains are intense* and *intermittent* and there be malaria it has also benefitted the disease. Favorable results have been observed in trachoma, with or without pannus, and corneal ulcer with iritis.

CHININUM SULPHURICUM—Chin. s.

Quinine Sulphate. $(C_{20}H_{24}N_2O_2)_2H_2SO_4.7HO_2$.

Objective.—Disc and retina very anæmic. Mydriasis. Lacrimation.

Subjective.—Photophobia. Neuralgic twinges in the supra- and infra-orbital nerves, usually periodic.

Clinical.—Optic neuritis is said to have been cured. Is homœopathic to anæmia (retinal, etc.), particularly if there is or was intermittent fever of distinct regular stages in the paroxysms.

CHLORALUM—Chloral

Chloral Hydrate.

Objective.—Conjunctival injection. Optic disc pale; or congested.

Subjective.—Eyes weak. Headache over both eyes, running down into the eyes, $<$ left side, with feeling as if the eyes were constricted.

Vision.—Dim. Circles of light. Black spots.

CICUTA MACULATA—Cic.

Spotted Water Hemlock.

Objective.—Eyes stare. Pupils dilated insensible; first contracted, later dilated. Lids tremble and twitch.

Subjective.—Eyes sensitive to light.

Vision.—Objects appear to alternately approach and recede. Diplopia, objects appear double.

Characteristics.—Extremely sensitive to touch or drafts which may excite (little) convulsions.

Clinical.—Useful in spasmodic affections of the eye and its appendages. *Strabismus,* periodic, spasmodic, after a fall or blow or each time the child is frightened.

CIMICIFUGA RACEMOSA—Cimic.

Actæa Racemosa. Black Cohosh. Black Snake Root.

Objective.—Mydriasis. Eyes congested during headache.

Subjective.—*Aching pain in the eyeballs; between ball and orbital plate of frontal bone; extending backward through base of brain to occiput.* Pain from eyes to top of head.

Vision.—Dark spots.

Characteristics.—Myalgia. Spinal irritation. Heat on vertex; "top of head will fly off."

Clinical.—Asthenopia and ciliary neuralgia, particularly if the symptoms are *reflex from uterus, ovaries or spine.*

CINA—Cina.

Wormseed (not wormwood).

(Its alkaloid is Santonin, $C_{15}H_{18}O_3$.)

Objective.—Convulsive pulsation of the supraciliary muscles. Mydriasis.

Subjective.—A slow stitch from above upper orbital margin deep into the brain.

Vision.—Chromopsia, yellow vision (and Santonin, the alkaloid). Optical illusion in bright colors. Black before the eyes on rising from bed, with dizziness and faintness; staggers; > lying down.

Clinical.—Has been useful in strabismus and other eye troubles due to helminthiasis in children of a pale, sickly appearance with blue rings around the eyes; also in asthenopia from refraction anomalies or presbyopia.

CINNABAR—Cinnab.

Mercuric (red) sulphid. HgS.

Objective.—Redness of the whole eye.

Subjective.—*Pain from lacrimal duct through brow to ear or temple. Pains from inner to outer corner of eye in the bone around edge of orbit,* usually above but sometimes below. *Drawing sensation from right inner canthus across the malar bone to the ear.* Shooting pains in right inner canthus, with burning and itching. Aching soreness in the eyes, < *evening.* Weakness and sleepiness in the eyes about noon, scarcely could keep them open.

Clinical.—An important remedy in blepharitis, conjunctivitis, keratitis, iritis and scleritis, even severe ulceration of the cornea, if accompanied by the characteristic pain through the brow or around the edges of the orbit; this pain may vary in character and intensity, may be sharp or aching and extend into the eye or head. It has been useful in syphilitic iritis with gummata. Pain, as with other mercury preparations, is < at night, usually < evening. Asthenopia. Ciliary neuralgia.

CLEMATIS ERECTA—Clem.

Virgin's Bower.

Objective.—Myosis. Eyes red and glittering, hot and dry. Inflammation of the whites.

Subjective.—Photophobia. Great sensitiveness to cold air, light and bathing. Biting burning in the eyes as if fire streamed out of them. Dryness and heat, compelling to close the lids. Smarting, rawness. Pain in middle of left eyeball. Pressure in orbits on moving the eyes.

Clinical.—Has been useful in iritis, kerato-iritis; scrofulous and mercurial affections.

COCCULUS INDICUS—Coccul.

Indian Cockle.

Objective.—Myosis. Lids inflamed. Sclera red, cornea hazy.

Subjective.—Bruised or pressive pains in eyes; hard to open lids, < night. Pain in eyes as if torn out of the head.

Vision.—Right hemianopsia: sees only left half of the line when reading.

Characteristics.—A prostrating nausea. The cerebro-spinal system is debilitated.

Clinical.—Asthenopic headaches, occiput and nape. Car sickness, sea sickness.

COLCHICUM AUTUMNALE—Colch.

Meadow Saffron.

Objective.—Inflamed eyes. Lacrimation, < open air. Lids in constant motion.

Subjective.—Violent tearing pains in the eyes.

Characteristics.—The smell of food is very repugnant, even to nausea.

Clinical.—Rheumatic gouty cases, particularly with debility; in this case beware of large doses.

COLOCYNTHIS—Coloc.

Bitter Apple.

Subjective.—Pains *screwing, sharp, cutting,* boring, > by pressure.

Clinical.—Neuralgia. Useful also in controlling the pains of iritis and glaucoma; there may be severe burning, sticking or cutting, extending from the eye into the head and around the eye, or else an aching pain going back into the head, usually < on rest at night and on stooping, > *firm pressure* and walking in a warm room. Sometimes there is on stooping a sensation as if the eye would fall out.

COMOCLADIA DENTATA—Como.

Guao. Bastard Brazil Wood.

Subjective.—*(Right) eye very painful, feeling much larger and more protruding than the left. < near a warm stove.* Eyes feel heavy; as if something were pressing on top of the balls, moving them downward and outward. < right. < motion. Eyeball aches terribly.

CONIUM MACULATUM—Con.

Poison Hemlock. Spotted Hemlock.

Objective.—White of the eye yellow. Pupils dilated and sluggish. Lacrimation. Lids droop. Ptosis. Paresis of the extrinsic muscles.

Subjective.—*Intense photophobia with little or no redness. Weakness and dazzling of the eyes with giddiness and debility, specially of the arms* *and legs so that on trying to walk he staggers as if drunk.* Pressure in the eyes, sleepy, while reading. Lids seem pressed down by a heavy weight. Burning in the eyes and lids. Smarting in the inner canthus, as from something corrosive.

Vision.—*Accommodation sluggish.* Vision good for fixed objects, but when the object is put in motion there is a haze and dimness of vision with vertigo. Diplopia. Objects waver.

Characteristics.—Conium is the first remedy when *photophobia or pain is excessive and out of all proportion to the amount of trouble; the nerves are hyperesthetic, their terminal filaments (in the cornea) are exposed by superficial abrasion.* Dizziness > closing the eyes.

Clinical.—One of the principal remedies for keratitis (ulcers, pustules) if the inflammation is superficial, involving only the epithelial layer, and caused by cold, trauma or scrofula. Hyperesthesia of the retina frequently calls for this remedy. In one such case (cured) *all colors appeared white;* photophobia was most intense, but external and internal examination of the eye revealed nothing abnormal.

CREOSOTUM—see Kreosotum.

CROCUS SATIVUS—Croc.

Saffron.

Objective.—Mydriasis. Visible twitches in the lids; upper lids. Must wink frequently.

Subjective.—Excessive photophobia. Inclined to press the lids tightly together from time to time. *Feeling in the eyes as after violent weeping.* Feeling as though water was constantly coming into the eyes, not when in the open air. After reading awhile, even during the day, eyes pain with sore burning and some dimness so that he was very frequently obliged to wink. Feeling as of biting smoke in the eyes.

Vision.—The light seems dimmer than usual, as if obscured by a veil. Frequently has to wipe and wink the eyes as though a film of mucus were over them. Photopsies—sudden flashes like electric sparks.

Characteristics.—*Sensation as if something were alive in the abdomen.*

Clinical.—Asthenopia. Ciliary neuralgia. Posterior sclerochoroiditis. And in other diseases: Pain in eye to top of head. Pain in left eye darting to the right. Sensation of a cold wind blowing across the eyes. Constant winking with the eyes suffused with tears.

CROTALUS HORRIDUS—Crotal.

Rattlesnake Venom.

Objective.—*Yellow color of the eyes.* Blue rings around the eyes. Blood exudes from the eyes. Aqueous humor cloudy. Redness of the eyes. Lacrimation.

Subjective.—Pressure above the eyes. Burning in the eyes.

Characteristics.—Like other snake poisons, disorganizes the blood; acts primarily upon the cerebrospinal nerve centers. Ecchymosis.

Clinical.—Crotalus is the great remedy for yellow fever (argentum nitricum is only second to it). Is used in ophthalmology principally for *intraocular hæmorrhages,* into the vitreous, but particularly for *non-inflammatory retinal hæmorrhages.*

CROTON TIGLIUM—Crot. tig.

Croton Oil.

Objective.—Conjunctivitis. Copious lacrimation. Lids edematous.

Subjective.—Violent pains in the eyes. Stinging in the eyeball. Eyes feel drawn backward. *Tensive pain above the right orbit.*

Clinical.—As might be expected from its action on the skin, croton oil is often of great service for vesicles and pustules on the eyeball or lids and in herpes zoster ophthalmicus.

CYCLAMEN EUROPÆUM—Cycl.

Sow Bread.

Objective.—Swelling of upper lids.

Subjective.—Eyes burn; dryness and pressure.

Vision.—*Dim, and spots, < on waking.* Dim vision as of smoke or fog. *Flickering of various colors.* Photopsia: sees countless stars; fiery specks, sparks, glittering needles. Flickering of the light, on trying to read.

Characteristics.—Strabismus from menstrual or gastric irregularities. Chlorotic anæmic women; torpid mind and body.

DIGITALIS PURPUREA—Dig.

Purple Fox Glove.

Objective.—Mydriasis. Lid margins red, swollen and agglutinated in the morning.

Subjective.—Slight photophobia.

Vision.—Objects appear *green or yellow.* Muscæ volitantes. While walking in the evening the *upper part of the visual field seemed covered by a dark cloud.*

Clinical.—Has been used for detachment of the retina.

DUBOISIA MYOPOROIDES—Dub.

Cork Wood Tree.

Objective.—*Mydriasis. Vessels of the disc much enlarged and tortuous. Retinal veins dilated and tortuous. Fundus very hyperæmic.* Arteries of the retina diminished in size. Lids slightly edematous; morning agglutination.

Subjective.—*Pain over eyeball just beneath the brow. Sharp pain in upper part of eyeball.* Eyes hot and dry; feel tired as if overworked.

Vision.—*Paralysis of accommodation,* sets in (from instillation) before the mydriasis and lasts longer.

Characteristics.—Marked *vertigo, particularly with pale face, not of gastric origin.* Duboisia may be differentiated from belladonna in that it has vertigo, is not spasmodic and does not have neuralgia.

Clinical.—Duboisia is of the most value in *retinal hyperæmia with weak accommodation. True weakness of accommodation.* Optic neuritis and retinitis. Chronic hyperæmia of the palpebral conjunctiva.

EUPATORIUM PERFOLIATUM—Eup. perf.

Boneset.

Subjective.—Photophobia. Great soreness of the eyeballs.

Clinical.—This drug has been useful when *excessive soreness of the balls* has been a prominent symptom, particularly in malarial patients of the eup. perf. type.

EUPHRASIA OFFICINALIS—Euph.

Eyebright.

Objective.—Conjunctival injection. *Lids, or their margins, swollen and red. Profuse acrid lacrimation.*

Subjective.—*Photophobia.* Eyes sensitive to candle light. *Frequent inclination to blink. Feeling as if cornea were covered with much mucus, which obscures vision and obliges him frequently to close and press the lids together.* Tears hot and biting. Lids burn and itch. Red margins feel dry. In the eye: burning, biting, itching, obliges frequent winking and wiping.

Vision.—*Sometimes dim, as through a veil, in the evening. Blurred vision > by wiping the eyes or winking.*

Characteristics.—Euphrasia resembles mercurius in acridity but *its discharges are thick and excoriating while those of mercury are thin and acrid.*

Clinical.—Important for superficial inflammations: blepharitis, catarrhal inflammation of conjunctiva and cornea, acute, particularly if there be bland coryza. Euphrasia has been occasionally used in muscular paresis.

FERRUM METALLICUM—Fer.

Iron by Hydrogen. Fe.

Objective.—Eyes watery, dull, confused. Red, with burning pains. Lids swollen, discharging profusely when opened.

Subjective.—Photophobia. Eyes ache as if they would protrude. Burning stinging pains in inflamed eyes. Stinging pain over left eye, comes suddenly and lasts but a short time.

Vision.—Dark before the eyes; giddy. Letters run together when reading or writing.

Characteristics.—Pale face, flushes readily. Erythistic anæmia. Chlorosis.

FERRUM PHOSPHORICUM—Fe. ph.

Ferroso-ferric phosphate, U. S. P., 1860.
Ferri phosphas albus.*

Objective.—Eyes injected, inflamed; red and sore looking. Styes.

Subjective.—Dryness and roughness of lids. *Feeling as if grains of sand were under the lids.*

**No. Am. Jour. of Hom.*, vol. 37, 1889, p. 218, or Trans. N. Y. State Hom. Med. Soc., 1889, p. 85.

Burning and soreness in the inflamed eyes. Pain in the ball, < moving the eye.

Characteristics.—First stage of inflammation; asthenic patients. (Aconite for the sthenic case.) The pulse, even in fever, is full soft, compressible (not intermittent like that of gelsemium).

Clinical.—Retinitis, acute conjunctivitis parenchymatous keratitis when there is excessive inflammation, and corneal abscess before hypopion. Great lacrimation and photophobia.

FLUORIC ACID—Fl. ac.

Hydrofluoric acid. HFl.

Subjective.—Sensation as if the lids were opened by force and *a fresh wind were blowing upon them;* after that, feeling of sand in the eye, which felt inflamed.

Clinical.—This italicised symptom has often been verified in various eye diseases.

GELSEMIUM SEMPERVIRENS—Gels.

Yellow Jessamine.

Objective.—*Lids droop.* Eyes half closed, apparent inability to move the lids. Lids close on looking steadily at anything. Lateral nystagmus, on using the eyes. Mydriasis. Pupil sluggish.

Subjective.—*Great heaviness of the lids.* Aversion to light. Soreness of the balls. Dull feeling (with some aching) in the whole of the orbits. Bruised pain above and back of the orbits. Drawing over the eyes. Pain from over eyes to occiput, < right. Orbital neuralgia.

Vision.—*Dim sight, with vertigo. Smoky appearance before the eyes, with pain over them.* Black and bright specks. Glimmering. Objects appear double. Diplopia which can be controlled by an effort of the will. Diplopia when inclining the head to either shoulder, but vision single when holding the head erect.

Clinical.—Gelsemium is valuable in paralysis and diseases of the fundus, but is rarely beneficial in superficial affections of the eyes. Its action is very marked in *serous uveitis or serous inflammation of the choroid, ciliary body or iris separately.* It has a reputation for *detached retina, glaucoma, serous iritis, "Descemetitis,"* the ball being slightly reddened, also in *retino-choroiditis and disseminate choroiditis.*

GLONOIN—Glon.

Nitroglycerine. $C_3H_5(NO_3)_3$.

Objective.—Mydriasis. Eyes rolled up. Eyes injected, protruding, look wild. Apoplexy of the retina, vessels distended.

Subjective.—Eyes feel too large and protrude as though bursting out of the head. Pressing protruding pains.

Vision.—Photopsies, sparks, flashes. Black spots on stooping. Objects dance with every pulse.

Characteristics.—A tendency to sudden and violent irregularities of the circulation. *Rush of blood to the head. Painless throbbing in the whole body, or in the brain.*

Clinical.—The great remedy for sun-stroke, for *heat prostration.* Eye troubles from exposure to very bright light. Supraorbital neuralgia.

GRAPHITES—Graph.

Graphite. Black Lead.

Objective.—*Very inflamed lid margins. Dry mucus in the lashes. Canthi crack and bleed easily. External canthus inflamed.* Morning agglutination. Thin excoriating mucopurulent discharge. Lacrimation. Redness of the whites. A stye on the lower lid.

Subjective.—Photophobia, intense in daylight rather than in artificial light. Light dazzles the eyes. Sense of dryness in the lids and pressure. Heaviness of lids. Heat about lids. Heat, burning, biting, smarting in the eyes.

Vision.—Vanishing of sight during menstruation. Flickering. When writing letters run together and appear double.

Clinical.—Few remedies are so frequently called for in chronic marginal blepharitis, in chronic inflammation of the lids, conjunctiva or cornea, in scrofulous subjects, particularly when there is intertrigo or eczema characterized by *moist cracks which bleed easily.* It has cured corneal ulcer, even with hypopion, but is more adapted to superficial ulceration from pustules, often with considerable vascularity of the cornea. Pustular keratitis. Morning <.

HAMAMELIS VIRGINICA—Ham.

Witch Hazel.

Objective.—Lids swollen. Eyes bloodshot.

Subjective.—Eyes feel forced out. Sore pain in the eye.

Characteristics.—The sphere of action of hamamelis is passive congestion, venous hæmorrhage.

Clinical.—Traumatic iritis with hæmorrhage; it has been of most service for *hastening the absorption of intraocular hæmorrhages.*

HEPAR—Hep.

Hepar sulphuris calcareum. Impure calcium sulphid. CaS.

Introduced by Hahnemann; made from calcined oyster shells and sulphur; should be made according to his directions. Calcium sulphid has not been proved, hence should not be used interchangeably with this, particularly in doses above the 1x.

Objective.—*Upper lid red, swollen, inflamed,* with pressive pain. Morning agglutination. Inflamed eyes, whites red. Profuse lacrimation. Spasmodically closed lids in the morning.

Subjective.—Intense photophobia. *Eyes very painful,* or ache, *in bright daylight, if he attempts to move them. Eyeballs very sensitive to touch.* Pains: sore as if beaten, pressive, throbbing, shooting, smarting. Smarting pain in external canthus, with hardened mucus. Pressure in eyes, as from sand.

Vision.—Obscuration while reading. Dim sight by candle light. Blindness on rising and standing after sitting bent over. Field of vision reduced one-half. Continual movement of bright circles before eyes. Objects look too large.

Characteristics.—*Oversensitiveness of the nervous system,* hence *extreme sensitiveness to touch, to cold air, and to cold applications;* the sensitiveness makes the subject *irritable with hasty speech and actions.*

Clinical.—One of the most frequently used eye remedies. *Acute phlegmonous inflammations; pustular and ulcerative keratitis with great intensity of symptoms; deep sloughing corneal ulcer with hypopion; corneal abscess; keratoiritis;* catarrhal or purulent conjunctivitis; parenchymatous keratitis; cyclitis; suppurative choroiditis; panophthalmitis. There is no better remedy to *hasten the absorption of pus,* as in hypopion, and for curing the suppurative process. It has been demonstrated that hepar can raise and lower the opsonic index. In the potencies it can abort threatened suppuration, but most commonly is given low, 1x, to hasten suppuration, "ripen" boils, and facilitate the discharge of pus. It acts upon the glandular system, is one of the great "scrofula" remedies. The fact that the patient has taken much mercury is an additional indication for hepar.

HYOSCYAMUS NIGER—Hyos.

Henbane.

Objective.—Eyes distorted. *Squinting. Staring.* Red; wild, sparkling; brilliant; and rolling about. *Pupils dilated* and insensible, and albuginea red. Conjunctiva injected.

Vision.—*Dim. Short. Small objects seem very large. Of two flames of equal size one seemed smaller, the other larger.*

Clinical.—Spasms of the ocular muscles, eyes distorted or rolling. Illusions of vision, objects seem large or double or indistinct.

HYPERICUM PERFORATUM—Hyper.

St. John's Wort.

Clinical.—"The arnica of the nerves." Relieves pain, and so facilitates recovery, after operations and accidents. Irritable scars. The author permanently relieved the irritability—recurrent congestion and pain—of an eye which had been blinded two or three years previously by a knife cut which left cataract and anterior synechiæ, with this remedy.

IGNATIA AMARA—Ign.

St. Ignatius' Bean.

Objective.—Constant winking with spasmodic action of various facial muscles. Lacrimation with the pain.

Subjective.—Photophobia, intense but fitful. Pain from head into left eye, when the eyes began to burn and water. Pressure in the eyes as from sand. Evening, pain in inner surface of the upper lid as if it were too dry. Sensation as of a particle in the left external canthus.

Vision.—Zigzag and serpentine white flickering at one side of the visual field.

Characteristics.—*Contradictoriness of symptoms and modalities.*

Clinical.—The usefulness of ignatia has been confined to nervous, hysterical patients. Cures have been reported of ciliary neuralgia, retinal hyperesthesia, conjunctivitis and corneal ulcer.

IODUM—Iod.

Iodine. I.

Objective.—Sclera dirty yellow. Eyes protrude. Lids edematous. Eyes inflamed as from taking cold.

Subjective.—Pain as from excoriation.

Characteristics.—*Although a ravenous eater the patient is painfully thin. The patient loves cold air, feels better in it.*

Clinical.—Iodine is to be thought of for *acute exacerbation of chronic inflammation.* Goiter; exophthalmic goiter. Catarrhal conjunctivitis. Acute dacryocystitis; the bluish red inflammation extends under the eye. The late Dr. John F. Gray recommended for acute phlegmonous dacryocystitis six drops of compound tincture of iodine in six ounces of water, a dram ("a swallow") taken every hour or two. The author has found the homœopathic tincture acts similarly and just as well.

IPECAC—Ipec.

Ipecacuanha.

Objective.—Myosis. Violent *conjunctivitis. Cornea dim, as if infiltrated; on close examination there were noticed a number of small depressions.* Profuse lacrimation; tears gush when lids are separated. Skin of lids red.

Subjective.—*Great photophobia.* Intense tearing or tensive pains in the eyes. Constant severe pain over the eyes, specially the left.

Vision.—Blue and red halo around the light.

Characteristics.—*Nausea* with clean tongue.

Clinical.—Very valuable in *phlyctenular* ophthalmia, phlyctenules or ulcers of conjunctiva or cornea; the cornea may be vascular. Much photophobia with redness.

JABORANDI—Jab.

Pilocarpus. (Its alkaloid is Pilocarpin.)

Objective.—*Myosis.* Lids twitch.

Subjective.—*Eyes tire from near vision.* Headache on using the eyes. Vertigo and *nausea on using the eyes.*

Vision.—*Near sighted; approximation of both far and near points. Spasm of accommodation while reading. The state of vision is constantly changing,* becomes suddenly more or less dim every few moments. *Everything at a distance hazy. Could read moderate size type at one but not at two feet. Nausea from looking at moving objects.* Spots before eyes.

Characteristics.—*Spasm of accommodation from irritable weakness of the ciliary muscle.* Primarily increased secretion; secondarily, dryness.

Clinical.—One of our valuable eye remedies. Norton recommends it for serous choroiditis and for recent periodic convergent squint not dependent upon weakness of the opposing muscle. The following symptoms have been repeatedly relieved: < moving the eyes; heat and burning, smarting and pain, in the eyes on using them.

KALI BICHROMICUM—Kali b.

Potassium dichromate. $K_2Cr_2O_7$.

Objective.—Dark rings about the eyes. Lid margins very red. Inflamed eyes with *yellowish stringy discharge* and morning agglutination. Conjunctiva injected, both of lids and ball. Small white conjunctival pustules. *Pustules on* *left cornea with surrounding indolent inflammation.* Lacrimation.

Subjective.—Heat and pressure in the eyes. Itching and burning. Eyes smart, < evening and open air. Heavy pain above the eyes, < on motion and from cold. Violent shooting pain from root of nose along left orbital arch to external angle of the eye exactly, with dim sight like a scale on the eye.

Characteristics.—*Discharges are viscid and stringy, yellow,* more or less purulent. *Ulcers tend to bore in without spreading laterally, they look as if punched out;* those in the cornea are *sluggish with very little or no redness and no photophobia.*

Clinical.—Usually pain and lacrimation are absent. The eye may be quite sensitive to touch. Opacities of the cornea, particularly if yellowish in hue, have been cleared. No other remedy has been so successful for uveitis, the old "Descemetitis" (not serous iritis) characterized by fine punctate opacities on Descemet's membrane, particularly over the pupil, and *with only moderate irritation of the eye.* This remedy is always to be thought of for chronic indolent inflammation of the eye, as above described, ulcers and pustules of the cornea or conjunctiva. It is also of great value in mild cases of croupous conjunctivitis in which the false membrane is loosely adherent, easily detached, and shows a tendency to roll up and separate into shreds which may give the discharge a stringy appearance. Profuse discharge, conjunctiva much inflamed, even to chemosis, lids swollen and maybe hazy cornea have been relieved.

KALI CARBONICUM—Kali c.

Potassium carbonate. K_2CO_3.

Objective.—*Swelling, puffiness, between brow and lid, like a sac.* White of eye red, injected. Lacrimation.

Subjective.—Photophobia. *Sharp* tearing in right orbit and in the eye at night. *Stitches* in the middle of the eye. Burning biting and pressure in the eyes. Pressure above the eyes. Soreness of external canthus with burning pain. Smarting pain in the eye. Eyes painful on reading.

Vision.—Bright sparks; blue or green spots. Weakness of vision.

Characteristics.—Backache, weakness and sweat. Pulse rapid and very weak or irregular, intermittent. Edema of the lids, especially if with *sticking pains.* An important cardiac remedy; $<$ 3 a. m.

Clinical.—Asthenopia. Weak sight from excessive sexual indulgence. Small round corneal ulcers without photophobia.

KALI IODATUM—Kali i.

Kali hydriodicum. Potassium iodid. KI.

Objective.—A diffuse keratitis developed during administration of pot. iod. and improved rapidly upon discontinuing the drug. Edema of the lids. Purulent conjunctivitis; chemosis. Lacrimation.

Subjective.—Eyes burn. Pain over left side of head and in the eye, < dark stormy days.

Vision.—Dim, foggy.

Characteristics.—When this remedy is thoroughly indicated there will almost always be an edematous or infiltrated state of the affected part.

Clinical.—Very useful for violent syphilitic iritis, after the abuse of mercury; iris is much swollen, aqueous cloudy, ciliary injection marked, a bright angry red. Pain, < at night, may be very severe. Photophobia and lacrimation variable. Has helped orbital periostitis, syphilitic or not, pain intense or absent. Pustules of cornea and conjunctiva. A very prominent remedy for acute or chronic iridochoroiditis, especially if syphilitic, with *excessive and variable amount of haziness of the vitreous.*

Kali iodatum is the first remedy thought of for paralysis of any muscle due to syphilitic periostitis.

When better proven it will be better possible to prescribe this remedy homœopathically and then smaller doses may be serviceable.

KALI MURIATICUM—Kali m.

Potassium chlorid. KCl.

There has been an unfortunate tendency to consider the chlorid and chlorate interchangeable therapeutically, and for druggists to substitute either for the other at their convenience. This should be strictly guarded against; they are not the same, chemically nor therapeutically.

Clinical.—(There are no provings.) Introduced by Schuessler who recommended it for the second, the exudative, stage in inflammations.

Characteristics.—*Indolent inflammation. Discharges thick whitish fibrinous mucus; dirty white or gray coat at base of tongue; fibrinous exudation in interstitial connective tissue;* lymphatic enlargements.

Has been found valuable for *parenchymatous keratitis;* and for asthenic corneal ulcer which generally begins near the limbus and extends toward the center with dirty white or yellow base, often very vascular and surrounded by considerable corneal infiltration, moderate mucous discharge. Tedious cases. Also for chorioretinitis with exudation. Discharge of white mucus or yellowish green matter from the eyes. Feeling of sand in the eye. Superficial flat ulcer "on the eye" from a vesicle. Blisters on the cornea. Onyx.

KALMIA LATIFOLIA—Kalm.

Mountain Laurel.

Subjective.—*Stiffness of muscles around eyes, and of the lids. Turning the eyes is painful.*

Vision.—Dim. Glimmering, at point of (near) fixation.

Clinical.—Ptosis, of rheumatic origin. Supraorbital neuralgia, < right. Scleritis. Sclerochoroiditis, anterior and posterior, sometimes with vitreous exudation. *Retinitis albuminurica,* specially during *pregnancy. Muscular asthenopia.*

KREOSOTUM—Kreos.

Creosote. Kreosote.

Clinical.—Blepharitis, and acute aggravations of chronic keratitis, with *profuse, hot, scalding, acrid lacrimation* early in the morning; blennorrhea (conjunctival) with moderately profuse discharge and much smarting in the eyes.

LACHESIS MUTUS—Lach.

(Erroneously Trigonocephalus.) The Bushmaster.

Subjective.—Eyes feel stiff. Pressure. Ache, especially the left. Stitches as from knives, in the eyes coming from the head. Sticking and drawing pain in and above the eyes. Eyes sensitive to light.

Vision.—Dim; *much black flickering,* that seems near, often making reading difficult. Fog before the eyes; in the evening a bluish-gray ring about six inches in diameter around the light. *Flickering,* as from threads or rays of the sun in zig-zag figures with congestion to head and headache, and jerking in right eye.

Characteristics.— < *left side. The patient sleeps into an aggravation.* < *morning after sleeping.* Sensitiveness of surface of body, particularly *cannot bear anything tight about the neck.* Cough excited or < by pressure on throat.

Clinical.—*Useful in absorbing intraocular hæmorrhages,* whether in anterior chamber, vitreous, retina or choroid. *Retinitis apoplectica.* Orbital cellulitis. Asthenopia. Phlyctenular keratitis, particularly the chronic recurrent form with superficial ulceration and moderate redness.

One of the chief remedies for climacteric flushes, particularly in run-down women. Like the other snake poisons, lachesis destroys the fibrin in the blood; the nerve centers are poisoned, particularly that of the pneumogastric.

LEDUM PALUSTRE—Led.

Wild Rosemary.

Objective.—Mydriasis. Acrid lacrimation.

Subjective.—Lids burn. Pressure (or dull pain) behind the eye as if it would be forced out.

Clinical.—Ecchymosis, spontaneous or traumatic, of lids or conjunctiva. Used locally and internally. Mosquito bites; *punctured wounds;* post-operative *intraocular hæmorrhage.* Asthenopia.

LILIUM TIGRINUM—Lil.

Tiger Lily.

Objective.—Lacrimation. Lid margins red.

Subjective.—Eyes burn, feel sandy on near vision; feel very weak. Eyes smart. Sharp pains over left eye. > in open air. Disposition to cover and press open the eyes. Retinal hyperesthesia.

Vision.—Blurred, with heat in eyes and lids, extending back into the head. Asthenopia. *Spasmodic astigmia. Spasm of accommodation.*

Characteristics.—The sphere of this remedy is

the female sexual, from which *the astigmia, ciliary spasm and the asthenopia are reflex.* Mental depression. Nervous irritability; hurried manner, desire to be busy.

LITHIUM CARBONICUM—Lith. c.

Lithium carbonate. Li_2CO_3.

Subjective.—Eyes pained, as if dry, during and after reading. Pain and heaviness over brows; < toward evening.

Vision.—*Right hemianopsia;* of two short words the right one is invisible. *Entire vanishing of whatever he looked at.*

Characteristics.—Rheumatic gout. *Tophi.*

Clinical.—Asthenopia.

LYCOPODIUM CLAVATUM—Lyc.

Club Moss.

Objective.—*Styes,* < toward inner canthus. *Ulceration and redness of lids,* with acrid lacrimation. Lids red and swollen, < toward night. Morning agglutination without redness. Purulent mucus. Must wipe mucus away to see clearly.

Subjective.—*Photophobia, < evening light. Tears smart and bite the cheek.* Severe burning and itching in eyes. Lids smart and burn. Lids dry, with smarting pain; difficult to open even on rubbing, in morning. Eyes dry and dim. Eyes dry in evening and night. Itching in both canthi with inflammation of right lids; *distressing pains as if they were dry,* with nightly agglutination. Pressive pain in eyes as from dust. Stitches in eyes.

Vision.—*Nyctalopia, night blindness. Evening light blinds him very much; can see nothing on the table.* Sensitive to daylight. Vision weak, unable to distinguish small objects as well as formerly. A veil and flickering before the eyes after the afternoon naps. Sees floating black spots, at a short distance. Right hemianopsia, same with one eye as with both, but < with the right. Sees only left half of an object distinctly.

Characteristics.— < *4 to 8 p. m.;* < *right side. Red sand in the urine.* Abdominal distension, *borborygmus, flatus. Early repletion when eating.* The patient likes sweets. Nutritional disorders. Gouty diathesis. Hæmorrhoids.

Clinical.—The progress of cataract has been arrested, when prescribed for chronic dyspeptic symptoms. Opacities of the vitreous have been known to disappear while taking lycopodium.

MAGNESIA PHOSPHORICA—Mag. phos.

Magnesium phosphate. $MgHPO_4.7H_2O$.

Objective.—Lids twitch. Lacrimation.

Subjective.—Orbital and supraorbital pains, < right side, > warm applications.

Clinical.—A spasmodic drug. Nystagmus. Spasmodic strabismus. Myosis. Diplopia. Photophobia. Chromotopsia, sparks. Is most used for neuralgia: the pains are paroxysmal, or shooting, darting, stinging, shifting, intermittent; always > by warmth and pressure.

MERCURIALIS PERENNIS—Mercurial.

Dog's Mercury.

Objective.—Eyes blink in open air and sunlight. Upper lids twitch, < left. Watery eyes. Mydriasis.

Subjective.—On waking at night unable to open eyes immediately; lids seemed paralyzed, could not be opened until she had rubbed them. Weakness of upper lids so that at times she could not completely raise them. *Lids heavy and dry; dryness of the eyes. Burning in the eyes.* Pain in eyes while reading and writing. Bruised sore feeling in eyes, with feeling as if they were too large for their sockets or as if they would be pushed out. Photophobia, to bright and artificial light.

Vision.—*Foggy, in morning. Letters run together while reading.*

Clinical.—*Asthenopia.* Conjunctival hyperæmia with heavy lids after near vision. This remedy should be considered oftener in asthenopia when the lids feel dry and heavy after near vision.

MERCURIUS—Merc.

Either Solubilis or Vivus. Either Hahnemann's Soluble Mercury or Quicksilver.

Objective.—*Upper lid thick and red,* like a stye. Eyes inflamed, with swollen tarsi, and very sensitive to touch or light. *Lids spasmodically closed. Acrid lacrimation.* Morning agglutination. *Eyes forcibly drawn together. Inflamed swelling in the region of the lacrimal bone.*

Subjective.—*Photophobia, fire, gas light; intolerance of light and fire-light.* Heat, redness, pressure, in the eyes, burning and biting. Sensation of a cutting substance under left upper lid.

Vision.—*Dim. A fog before one or both eyes. Eyes drawn together on trying to look at anything, can not see it distinctly;* the more she tries the less able is she to restrain the contraction, she is obliged to lie down and close the eyes. Muscæ volitantes. *Blinded by fire-light, in the evening.*

Characteristics.—< *at night. Discharges thin*

and acrid. < by the glare of a fire; < by warmth in general; < in bed at night.

Clinical.—One of the prominent eye remedies. Syphilis is a marked, but not a necessary, indication; the aggravations are of prime importance. Dacryocystitis. Syphilitic lacrimal fistula. Eye trouble from working over a fire. Ophthalmia neonatorum. Superficial inflammation of cornea or conjunctiva, catarrhal, phlyctenular or ulcerative. The corneal ulcer is usually quite vascular, it may be surrounded by a grayish opacity and accompanied by onyx. Conjunctival redness variable, usually marked; sometimes chemosis. Keratitis parenchymatosa, usually from hereditary syphilis. Kerato-iritis, with or without hypopion. Episcleritis. Mercurius pains are generally severe, more frequently tearing, burning, shooting or sticking, and not confined to the eye but extend into the forehead and temples. Temples often sore to touch. *Iritis, plastic,* gummatous. Retinitis. Choroiditis. Optic neuritis.

MERCURIUS BINIODATUS—Merc. bin.

Mercurius iodatus ruber. The red iodid. Mercuric iodid. HgI_2.

Clinical.—Has been useful in trachoma and pannus, corneal ulcer, scrofulous ophthalmia, diphtheritic conjunctivitis. The iodine seems relatively the more active element. Indurated cervical glands. Enlarged inflamed tonsils. The sore throat begins or is worse on the left side; it is more intense than with the yellow iodid.

MERCURIUS SUBLIMATUS CORROSIVUS—Merc. cor.

Corrosive sublimate. Mercuric chlorid. $HgCl_2$.

Characteristics.—The most active preparation of mercury, is characterized by the intensity of its symptoms; erythistic inflammation.

Clinical.—Is usually more useful than the solubilis for *scrofulous ophthalmia.* The sublimate seems to have a selective action upon the fundus oculi. No other remedy has been more frequently successful in *retinitis albuminurica,* because it may be a cause of, and is very successful in, albuminuric nephritis.

MERCURIUS DULCIS—Merc. dulc.

Calomel. Mercurous chlorid. Hg_2Cl_2.

Clinical.—Useful in ciliary blepharitis, phlyctenular and scrofulous ophthalmia. Selected usually on its general symptoms; sore nose and swollen upper lip are suggestive. Flabby, bloated, pallid subjects with glandular swellings. The liver is almost always involved.

MERCURIUS NITRICUS—Merc. nit.

Nitrate of mercury. $Hg(NO_3)_2$.

Clinical.—For pustules, ulcer and *phlyctenules of the cornea, particularly if recurrent,* try this unless something else internally is indicated—the 3 to 6 centesimal.

MERCURIUS PROTOIODATUS—Merc. prot.

Mercurius iodatus flavus. The yellow iodid. Mercurous iodid. Hg_2I_2.

Characteristics.—The mercury seems the more active element. There is a *thick dirty yellow coating at the base of the tongue.* Bad breath. Sore throat begins or is worse on the right side.

Clinical.—*Trachoma with pannus,* in all stages, but particularly for an acute exacerbation after the first stage has passed. *Corneal ulcer.* Particularly effective for *superficial ulceration of all or part, specially the upper part, of the cornea, commencing at the margin. Serpigenous ulcer.* One of the most prominent remedies for *corneal ulceration in the course of pannus and granular conjunctivitis.* Pustular conjunctivitis. Pustular keratitis. Iridochoroiditis. Opacities of the vitreous. Syphilitic paralysis of the oculomotor nerve. Syphilitic iritis. Syphilitic blepharitis. Blennorrhea of the lacrimal sac.

MEZEREUM—Mez.

Mezereon.

Objective.—*Obstinate twitches in the left upper lid.* Eyes inflamed on rising in the morning; conjunctiva injected, dirty red, $<$ left, $<$ near external canthus. Lacrimation.

Subjective.—*Eyes feel dry,* hot, with pressure. Pains in the eyes, pressing or tearing. Biting, smarting, with the lacrimation, must rub the eye. Itching of lid margin and skin near the nose.

Characteristics.—The chief use of this remedy is for syphilitic cases (abused with mercury) and scrofulosis of skin, periosteum, bones; and neuralgia. *Eczema, hard thick whitish yellow crusts with thick yellow pus under them, exuding on pressure,* is characteristic of this remedy. In *ciliary neuralgia* the pains radiate and shoot downward; there is a feeling as though cold air were blowing in the eye. Bones of the face feel sore. *The parts feel numb after the pain. Facial neuralgia involving the eye.*

NAPHTHALINUM—Naph.

Naphthalin. $C_{10}H_8$.

Objective.—This drug has caused in animals, cataract, detachment of the retina and, from smaller doses, small brilliant points in the optical papilla and also aggregated as a large white plaque, usually below the disc, which in extending covered over the choroidal vessels. The cataract, when developed more slowly from the smaller doses, began as a turbidity extending rapidly from the posterior surface and borders; there were also opaque radiating striæ from the borders of the lens.

NATRUM ARSENICOSUM—Nat. ars.

Sodium arsenate. $Na_2HAsO_4.7H_2O$.

Objective.—Palpebral and orbital conjunctiva much congested. Orbital edema, specially supra-orbitally. Morning agglutination. Lid edges chronically inflamed. Inner surface of (lower) lids granulated.

Subjective.—Photophobia, < at night. Lids disposed to close, to protect the weak eye; can not open them as wide as usual. Whole eye feels dry and painful; soon tires on near vision. Eyes smart as from wood smoke; smarting and lacrimation on going into open air. Burning lacrimation. Aching through and over brows and orbits, and in temples on awakening. Eye symptoms < morning, > evening.

Characteristics.—This salt resembles natrum muriaticum in its action more than it does arsenicum.

Clinical.—*Trachoma, with pannus.* Chronic catarrhal conditions: conjunctivitis, granular lids.

NATRUM CARBONICUM—Nat. c.

Sodium carbonate. $Na_2CO_3.10H_2O$.

Objective.—*Small ulcers of the cornea.* Lids involuntarily close, difficult to open.

Subjective.—Photophobia. Stinging pains with ulcers. Needle-like stitches in both eyes after dinner. Lids heavy.

Vision.—Dim; constantly obliged to wipe the eyes. Muscæ volitantes when writing. Dazzling flashes on waking.

Characteristics.—> by gentle rubbing.

Clinical.—Ulcerative keratitis. Small phlyctenules or ulcers of cornea with stinging pains and great photophobia.

NATRUM MURIATICUM—Nat. m.

Sodium chlorid. NaCl.

Objective.—Edges of lids red, inflamed; morning agglutination with crusts. *Irritability of lid margins, and their conjunctiva.* Spasmodic closure of the lids. *Acrid lacrimation which makes the canthi sore and red.* Lacrimation in open air; and inflammation with every slight wind.

Redness of the white of the eyes, with lacrimation; with feeling as if the balls were too large and compressed. Increased secretion of clear mucus, and of the sebaceous glands.

Subjective.—Lid margins burn, sore, feel inflamed. Eyes sensitive to light, smart and burn. *In the morning sensation of sand in the eyes.* Pains as from a foreign body. Dry feeling in the eyes as after weeping a long time, while riding in a carriage. Violent burning in the evening. Sticking in the right eye. Itching; smarting pain. Itching of inner canthi with lacrimation. Slight pressive pains over the eyebrows.

Vision.—*Pressure in the eyes on looking intently at anything.* Vision dim, eyes weak; misty all day; vision not as clear as usual. Objects seem covered with a thin veil. On looking at anything, specially on sewing, sudden darkness; she could see nothing until she directed her eyes at another object, at 6 p. m., with sleepiness. *Eyes give out on using them, at near or distant vision. Letters and stitches run together,* so that she can not distinguish anything for five minutes. *Unsteadiness of vision; objects become confused on looking at them.* Small *fiery points* wherever she looks.

Characteristics.—*Drawing stiff sensation in the eye-muscles on moving them. Morning aggra-*

vation, between 10 and 11 a. m.; *mental depression, melancholia; backache,* > *lying upon something hard; emaciation, of the neck disproportionate to that of the body.* Muscular weakness, particularly *of the internal recti. Frontal headache.*

Clinical.—Acts best, when indicated, in the higher potencies. Retinal images retained. Heat and a feeling as if there was a rush of blood to the eyes. Severe pain over right internal rectus. Use of eyes brings on heaviness and drooping of the lids, and aching of the balls. *Sharp pain over the eyes on looking down.*

Has proven beneficial in: *muscular asthenopia; follicular conjunctivitis,* chronic and mostly confined to the oculopalpebral folds, also when complicated with true trachoma; old cases of granular lids, with or without pannus; *pustules and ulcers of the cornea,* particularly if chronic and recurrent; retinal hyperesthesia; blenorrhea, profuse clear mucus; lacrimal stricture and fistula; ciliary neuralgia which comes and goes with the sun.

NATRUM SULPHURICUM—Nat. s.

Glauber's salt. Sodium sulphate.

$Na_2SO_4.10H_2O$.

Objective.—Morning agglutination. Lacrimation.

Subjective.—Photophobia. Eyes sensitive to light, with headache. Eyes weak. Burning, of right eye, of lid margins. Edges of lids itch in morning. Eyes pain in evening when reading by artificial light, with heaviness of lids.

Vision.—Dim. < near fire.

Characteristics.—The typical remedy for patients with the hydrogenoid constitution (Grauvogl): they can not tolerate sea air, they feel every change from dry to wet. Ailments dependent upon or aggravated by dampness of the weather or living in damp houses. Sycosis: latent gonorrhea.

Clinical.—Granular conjunctivitis. Locally it has seemed to help macula corneæ.

NITRIC ACID—Nit. ac.

HNO_3.

Objective.—Yellowness about the eyes with red cheeks. Lids swollen, hard. Difficulty in raising upper lids in morning. Lacrimation.

Subjective.—*Photophobia.* Burning, smarting, biting and *stitches* in the eye *like splinters.*

Vision.—*Double vision of horizontal objects,* at a distance. *Obscuration of sight while reading.* Short sighted; objects indistinct at a moderate distance. She can clearly distinguish nothing at night—nyctalopia—and everything seems double.

Characteristics.—Sensation as if a fish-bone, splinter or piece of glass were sticking in. The chief remedy in (mercurialized) secondary syphilis.

Clinical.—Keratitis; corneal ulcer, tending to perforate. Syphilitic iritis, chronic cases, nightly pain absent or usually mild; sometimes the pain is $<$ in the day than the night.

NUPHAR LUTEUM—Nuph.

Small Yellow Pond Lily.

Subjective.—Dull pain and sensation of weight in the orbit.

Vision.—Brilliant sparks, especially after hard coughing.

NUX MOSCHATA—Nux m.

Nutmeg.

Objective.—Blue rings around the eyes. Ptosis.

Subjective.—*Sensation of dryness in the eyes;* of fullness; can move lids only with difficulty; lids feel heavy and stiff; reading by artificial light is difficult, *the eyes would close from sleepiness.*

Vision.—*Objects appear too large.*

Characteristics.—*Sleepiness with all com-*

plaints. Dryness, of mouth, tongue and lips, without thirst. Functional disturbance from overtaxing the mind. Faintness or momentary unconsciousness. Hysteria.

Clinical.—Episcleritis has been cured with this remedy.

NUX VOMICA—Nux.

Poison Nut. Quaker Buttons.

Objective.—Lids twitch. Eyes blink. Movement difficult on account of muscular stiffness. Lacrimation; in morning, while yawning, eyes full of water.

Subjective.—*Photophobia,* < morning. *A smarting dry feeling in inner canthi, in the morning in bed.* Biting in the eyes, < external canthi, as from salt, with lacrimation. The canthi are painful as if sore. Margin of lid painful as if rubbed sore, < on touch, < *morning.* Pressure in the upper lids, and *in the margins.*

Vision.—*Cloudy.* Glittering appearance before the eyes; floating black and gray points. Vision very sensitive. Retinal hyperesthesia.

Characteristics.—Thin, *irritable, choleric* persons, with dark hair; persons who make great mental exertion, or *lead a sedentary life; debauchers who are irritable and thin. Worse in the morning.* Dull frontal headache (as from a cold or constipation). In the beginning of a cold when one is *chilly, aching, yawny, and stretchy.*. Nausea. Indigestion, soon after eating, from overeating, high living. Effects of tobacco, alcohol, drugging. *Constipation, teasing ineffectual desire for stool. Diarrhea, preceded by pain which is relieved by the passage.*

Clinical.—The special sphere of usefulness in ophthalmology is *acute and chronic retrobulbar neuritis, and atrophy of the optic nerve.* Amblyopia; amaurosis. Muscular paresis and paralysis. Ulcers, pustules, of the cornea. Iritis; chorioretinitis. Old cases of trachoma, even with pannus. Ciliary blepharitis; dacryocystoblennorrhea; blepharospasm; morbid nictitation.

ONOSMODIUM VIRGINIANUM—Onos.

False Gromwell. Gravel Weed.

Objective.—Optic disc hyperæmic and retinal vessels engorged, < left eye.

Subjective.—*Heaviness and dullness of the eyes.* Eyes feel as if they had lost much sleep. Lids heavy. Tense drawing and tired feeling in the ocular muscles. It is disagreeable to look at near objects. Eyes feel as if they were very wide open, and he wanted to look at distant objects. Pain in upper portion of left orbit with a feeling of expansion. Pain in and over the left eye. Dull heavy pain in and soreness of the eye-balls.

Vision.—Blurred. Far off objects look large.

Characteristics.—*Pains in left side of head and over left eye,* extending around left side to back of head and neck. *Dull heavy pains in occiput pressing upward with dizziness. Great muscular prostration, tired feeling all over the body. Muscles feel unsteady, treacherous, as if one dare not trust them to move.* < left side.

Clinical.—One of our very best medicines for *muscular asthenopia, and headache from eye-strain.*

OPIUM—Op.

Poppy.

Objective.—*Myosis.* Eyes half closed, red.

Subjective.—Eyes dry, weak, burn, and feel as if dust were in them. Sensation as if eyes were too large for their orbits.

Vision.—Scintillations.

Characteristics.—Great drowsiness.

Clinical.—Seldom used. May be studied for effects of fright, and in cerebral paralysis, or convulsions. Embolism of the central artery of the retina: one case (T. F. Allen) gradually recovered vision (and power in the paralyzed parts) under the use of opium alone.

OSMIUM—Os.

Os.

Objective.—Veins of fundus large and tortuous. Profuse lacrimation. Lids spasmodically closed, with the sharp orbital pain.

Subjective.—Sharp pain in orbit. Burning pain in eyes, with profuse lacrimation.

Vision.—*Halo around candle flame, rainbow,* bluish green or yellow. At a distance candle flame seems enveloped by dust or smoke. Dim sight. Letters run together, as from a fog.

Clinical.—One of the prominent remedies for *glaucoma,* which it has actually cured.

PARIS QUADRIFOLIA—Paris.

Herb Paris. Fox Grape. Four Leaved Grass.

Objective.—Jerking and twitching of right upper lid.

Subjective.—Eyes feel heavy. Eyeballs seem too large. Some stitches through the middle of the eye.

Clinical.—*Pain in the eyes as if pulled into the head; feeling as if threads drew the eye into the middle of the head, or pain drawing from the eye to the occiput.* This symptom has been repeatedly confirmed. Neuralgic headache, eyes feel projecting and a thread drawing them backward to middle of head. A case of paralysis of the iris and ciliary muscle was permanently cured with paris.

PETROLEUM—Petr.

Coal Oil. Rock Oil.

Objective.—An inflamed swelling (large as a pigeon's egg) in the inner canthus (like incipient lacrimal fistula). Epiphora. Conjunctivitis. Blepharoadenitis.

Subjective.—Burning and pressure in inner canthus. Itching and dryness of the lids. Itching and sticking in the eyes.

Vision.—Dim on exerting the eyes. Weak visual power.

Characteristics.—Tendency to fistula. Occipital headache. Rough dry skin with tendency to rhagades, cracks which bleed, suppurate; $<$ winter.

Clinical.—Suppurative dacryocystitis and *fistula. Marginal blepharitis.* Is sometimes indicated in: trachoma with pannus; scrofulous ophthalmia; iritis; blenorrhea of the lacrimal sac.

PHOSPHORIC ACID—Ph. ac.

H_3PO_4.

Clinical.—Has been useful in *frontal headaches of school children from over-use of the eyes;* asthenopia from nervous debility; neurasthenia.

PHOSPHORUS—Phos.

P.

Objective.—Eyes sunken and surrounded with blue rings. Eyes seem large. Edema of lids, and around the eyes. Ptosis. Myosis.

Subjective.—Aching and burning pains in the eyes. Stiffness and heat. Dull pain after reading.

Vision.—*Objects look red. Letters look red, when reading. Hemeralopia—day-blindness—sees more distinctly in twilight than during the day.* Eyes give out while reading. Obliged to hold objects near to see them distinctly; at a distance everything seems enveloped in a fog or mist; could see better when pupils were dilated by shading them with the hand. Dimness, cloudy vision. Everything seems in a mist. Seems as if there were a black veil before the right eye. A green halo about the candle light in the evening. Photopsies, sparks in the dark. Flickering before the eyes and roaring in the head. Muscæ volitantes, spots, points, dark objects in the vision.

Characteristics.—Irritable weakness of the nervous system. Very sensitive to external impressions, or the patient has been so. Makes the blood more liquid, slower in coagulating. Produces local stasis, and fatty degeneration. Small wounds bleed easily; brittle blood-vessels.

Clinical.—One of the principal remedies for deep-seated affections of the eye. Hyperæmia and inflammation of the optic nerve, retina and choroid. *Retinitis apoplectica; albuminurica;* with suppression of menses or other uterine or ovarian disorder. *Cataract. Glaucoma. Cherry-red color before the eyes.* Blindness after lightning stroke. Amblyopia. Asthenopia.

PHYSOSTIGMA VENENOSUM—Physos.

Calabar Bean.

Objective.—*Myosis. Twitches of lids.* Lacrimation.

Subjective.—*Twitching in the ball. Drawing twisting sensation in the eyes.* Eyes sore and painful when moved from side to side. Intolerable pain over both orbits. Pain in eyeballs, sharp, shooting. Dull pain over or between the eyes, after use. Eyes smart; lids feel sore; heavy. Aching in posterior part of orbit, extending back into brain, < reading, causes nausea. Eyes sensitive to light; feel weak.

Vision.—*Spasm of accommodation,* this may be *irregular* and cause *astigmia.* Blurred vision, a film; objects mixed. *The interni do not work right, the axes differ.*

Characteristics.—After local instillation, the accommodation recovers before the pupil does.

Physostigma can cause a perfect picture of spinal irritation.

Clinical.—Myopia, due to or increased by ciliary spasm, has been reduced perceptibly with the 2x internally.

PHYTOLACCA DECANDRA—Phyto.

Poke. Pigeon Berry.

Objective.—Lids inflamed, swollen, hard, reddish blue, edematous. < left, and in morning. Lids agglutinated. Lacrimation.

Subjective.—Photophobia. *Pressure around the eyes, in afternoon, as if they were too large.* Smarting, sandy, feeling in the eyes. Lids feel as if granulated and their edges feel scalded, hot, as if raw. Dull aching pains in the eyes, < motion, light or exercise. Aching pains along lower half of right orbit.

Characteristics.—Weakness. Tired aching and soreness general all over the body. *Stony hardness* of the *bluish inflammation* of cellular tissues.

Clinical.—*Orbital cellulitis, lids hard, swollen,* reddish blue, without severe pain; chemosis; more or less dull aching pain. Panophthalmitis; suppurative choroiditis; blepharitis. Has been useful in primary and secondary syphilis, and in malignant ulcers of the lids, as lupus, and epithelioma.

PICRIC ACID—Pic. ac.

$C_6H_2(NO_2)_3OH$.

Objective.—Yellow sclera. *Conjunctivitis, > cold air and washing with cold water, < in warm room, with difficulty in keeping eyes open.* Morning agglutination on waking.

Subjective.—*Sticky sensation on reading.* Feeling of sticks in the eyes. Dryness and sensation of sand. On studying, lids heavy, can not keep them open.

Vision.—Dim and confused; as if looking through a veil; air looks smoky. Sparks before the eyes, objects whirl.

Characteristics.—Brain fag. Neurasthenia. Mental or physical prostration on exertion. Spinal and cerebral irritation to depression and paralysis.

Clinical.—Dim vision, from neurasthenia, brain fag or sexual weakness.

PLANTAGO MAJOR—Plant.

Plantain.

Clinical.—*Ciliary neuralgia, prosopalgia, from decayed teeth.* Dull heavy ache in (left) eyeball with exquisite tenderness.

PLUMBUM METALLICUM—Plumb.

Lead. Pb.

Objective.—Mydriasis. Hypopion. *Sclera yellow; conjunctiva yellow. Optic neuritis;* papilla swollen, showed **post-mortem** interstitial hyperplasia of connective tissue, sheaths of optic nerve distended by fluid, cerebrospinal fluid increased, brain substance anæmic and the gray part yellowish. Disc prominent opaque, bluish-white, its outline hazy.

Vision.—*Dim. Diplopia.*

PRUNUS SPINOSA—Prun.

Blackthorn.

Subjective.—*Pain in the (right) eyeball as if inner part of the eye would be torn out. A sharp pain shooting like lightning from the right forehead through the brain* and coming out at the occiput.

Characteristics.—Neuralgia: *usually pressing asunder pains,* crushed or shooting; usually < motion, may be < night; occasionally periodic. Prunus relieves these pains and even the pathological condition which they accompany.

Clinical.—*An intense pain as if the eyeball must burst. Or, as if pressing asunder;* or as if crushed or wrenched. The pain is often sharp and shooting, may be above the eye extending into and around it or over the corresponding side of the head; sometimes shoots from behind the ear forward to the eye. *Ciliary neuralgia. Scleroticochoroiditis posterior,* other choroiditis with or without retinal complication, iridochoroiditis; iridocyclitis; haziness and opacities of the vitreous. Glaucoma.

PULSATILLA—Puls.

Wind Flower.

Objective.—*Hordeolum; with inflammation of the white,* now in one now in the other canthus. *Margin of lower lid inflamed and swollen, with lacrimation in the morning. Morning agglutination. An inflamed spot on the white near the cornea. Lacrimation* in the cold open air.

Subjective.—*Itching (biting) and burning in the lids in evening. Burning and itching in the eyes that provokes rubbing and scratching.* In inner canthus, pressive, biting, pains, sensation of soreness. Dryness of lids, of eye and sensation in morning of foreign body. Pressive burning pain in eyes; heat. Pressure as from sand when reading.

Vision.—*Dim; foggy. During the menses it became black before the eyes, < going into a warm room. Dizzy obscuration after sitting on* *rising and beginning to walk about.* Dark before the eyes in morning on rising from bed. Transient obscuration. Vision obscured with nausea and pale face.

Characteristics.—*A mild, gentle, tearful patient,* usually a blonde, often a female. Amenorrhea, scanty or delayed menses. May be irritable —but is amenable to reason. To *negroes* give pulsatilla if no other remedy is clearly indicated. < *warmth,* > *gentle motion in cool open air. Vertigo. Fever without thirst, even when the patient licks his lips to moisten them.* The *characteristic (mucous) discharge is bland, profuse, yellow* or whitish and thick. Indigestion; from rich, fat food; two or three hours after eating.

Clinical.—A valuable remedy, frequently called for; its selection should be largely governed by the temperament and general symptoms.

Catarrhal conjunctivitis; acute. Acute phlegmonous dacryocystitis, sometimes will be aborted. Trachoma without pannus. Blepharitis. *Styes;* if given early and not too strong often aborts them, and if continued prevents their recurrence. *Purulent conjunctivitis. Scrofulous ophthalmia; phlyctenular conjunctivitis* or keratitis; photophobia may be lacking. Superficial small corneal ulcers, from phlyctenules, often near middle of cornea. Episcleritis. Idiopathic iritis. Hyperæmia of the choroid, but more serviceable in hyperæmia of the optic nerve and retina. Has cured accommodative asthenopia.

RADIUM—Rad.

Radium bromid. $RaBr_2$.

Objective.—Ptosis. Dryness. Conjunctivitis. Yellow discharge. Muscular weakness, paretic.

Subjective.—Feeling of dryness. Eyes feel sticky. Ache. Shooting pains.

Characteristics.—Mental depression. General lassitude. All provers showed lowered blood-pressure, which persisted for some time, and also a marked increase of the phagocytic polymorphonuclear neutrophiles of the blood.

Increased elimination of urinary solids, particularly of the chlorids.

< motion; late afternoon; heat is disagreeable.

> continued motion; open air; pressure.

Clinical.—Functional disorders from disturbed metabolism. Rheumatism; gout. Neuralgia; neuritis. Nervous debility. Arteriosclerosis.

Cowperthwaite says that radium should prove to be a valuable intercurrent remedy, as it seems to increase the activities of other indicated remedies.

RANUNCULUS BULBOSUS—Ran. b.

Buttercup.

Subjective.—Violent pressing pains, at times in one at times in the other eyeball. Burning soreness in right lower lid. Smarting and soreness in right outer canthus. Sore smarting within (right) eye. Painfulness of right eyeball.

Vision.—Misty.

Characteristics.—Always < *damp weather,* or from change of temperature.

Clinical.—Herpes zoster ophthalmicus (bluish black vesicles) with violent pains in and above the eyes.

RHODODENDRON CHRYSANTHEMUM—Rhod.

Golden Flowered Rhodendron. *German,* Alpenrose. Schneerose.

Objective.—Mydriasis.

Subjective.—Dryness. Burning, periodical, in the eyes; without inflammation. Heat, burning pain, on near vision.

Characteristics.—A rheumatic remedy. The characteristic is < *at the approach of a storm and better after the storm breaks.*

Clinical.—*Muscular asthenopia, insufficiency of the interni.* Ciliary neuralgia. Glaucoma.

RHUS TOXICODENDRON—Rhus.

Poison Ivy. Three-leaved Ivy.

Objective.—*Lids inflamed, much swollen; upon opening them tears or pus gush out.* Lid puffy, relaxed with hot flushed face. A hard red swelling like a stye on left lower lid near inner canthus, with pressive pain. *Eyes inflamed; agglutinated in morning with matter. Lids heavy and stiff as if paralyzed,* difficult to move them. Burning pain, in evening, with *lacrimation. Whole eye and surroundings inflamed and swollen; lids erysipelatous with scattered watery vesicles; edematous.* Chemosis.

Subjective.—*Very sore around right eye. Ball very sore on turning or pressure, can hardly turn it. Violent itching,* pricking, burning in the swollen lids, and eyes. Eyes ache, or itch, on exerting them. Pressive pain as from dust or sand in the eye. Sharp pains from eyes into head. Drawing and tearing in region of brows and malar bones. Left eye felt enormously swollen and enlarged. Biting, as something sharp, acrid, were in the right eye.

Vision.—Great obscurity. A veil, could not see well. Extreme confusion of sight. Diplopia.

Characteristics.—*Restless (aching). > continued motion of affected parts despite stiff pain on beginning to move. > warmth; < in wet weather, < getting wet; < after midnight; < rest.*

Clinical.—The great remedy for *orbital cellulitis,* but particularly for *panophthalmitis; for the latter give tincture (then 1x) a few drops in a glass of water, two-dram doses repeated hourly if necessary.*

Epiphora, blepharitis, erysipelas, conjunctivitis, ptosis, ophthalmia neonatorum; pustules, ulcers of the cornea; *suppuration of the cornea following cataract extraction. Iritis, suppurative, rheumatic* or idiopathic. *Suppurative uveitis* (as above). Paresis or paralysis of any of the ocular muscles, intrinsic or extrinsic, *following exposure to cold and getting wet.*

RUTA GRAVEOLENS—Ruta.

Rue.

Objective.—Eye fills with water.

Subjective.—Pressure deep in the orbits. Pain as from a bruise in the tarsal cartilages. *Pressure over the brows.* Stitches in left frontal bone, only while reading. Itching in inner canthi and lower lids that after rubbing became a biting so that the eye filled with water. *Eyes burn, ache, feel strained from overtaxing them in near vision. Sensation of heat, fire, in eyes and aching, while reading.* Weary pain in eyes after reading. Coldness beneath left eye.

Vision.—*Blurred, from overtaxing in near vision. Very weak, as if eyes were excessively strained.* Objects dim as if a shadow flitted over them.

Characteristics.—In rheumatic subjects or after trauma to bones, joints, muscles. < cold wet weather, > motion, with a general feeling of soreness as from a bruise (backache).

Clinical.—Of the first importance in asthenopia, more often from *weakness of the ciliary muscle* than of the internal recti. *Heat and aching in and over the eyes,* which feel as if they were *balls of fire;* < night. Letters run together.

SANGUINARIA CANADENSIS—Sang.

Blood Root.

Objective.—Mydriasis. Eyes red, in morning. Lacrimation.

Subjective.—Burning dryness; followed by copious lacrimation. Pain over the eyes. Pain in balls on moving them. Balls sore, with darting through them and dim vision. Eyes > hard pressure on them.

Vision.—Dim.

Characteristics.—A tissue irritant. Anxiety is almost always present, but not as an isolated symptom. Circulatory disturbances. Sick headache, spreads from occiput over the head and settles over the right eye.

Clinical.—Acute conjunctivitis, and blepharoadenitis have been relieved.

SECALE CORNUTUM—Sec.

Ergot.

Objective.—*Eyes sunken and surrounded with a blue margin. Fixed, wild, staring.* Mydriasis. Cataract.

Vision.—Dim.

Characteristics.—> *from cold air.* < *applied heat.* Formication.

Clinical.—Cannot bear any covering or warmth—Ergot is one of the drugs that has caused cataract. It has been suggested for retinitis diabetica.

SENEGA—Sen.

Seneca Snake Root.

Objective.—Eyes watery.

Subjective.—Aching over the orbits. Dull aching oppressive pain about the eyes. Drawing and pressure in the balls, with lessened visual power. Dryness, with feeling as if the balls were too large for the orbits. Eyes weak, with much smarting, burning and lacrimation.

Vision.—Objects look shaded. Flickering when reading, obliging one to wipe the eyes often. Eyes tremble and water on looking intently at an object; weak and watery, or burn, when reading. Reading difficult because it makes the eyes feel dazzled. Flickering and running together of letters when reading. When walking toward the setting sun he seemed to see *another, smaller, sun below the first, assuming a somewhat oval shape when looking down, disappearing on bending the head backward.**

Clinical.—Senega is valuable for *absorption of lens fragments* after cataract operation or injuries. Hypotropia.

SEPIA—Sep.

Cuttle Fish Ink.

Objective.—*Lacrimation morning and evening;* in the open air. Lids droop, with the dull headache. Agglutination. *A red herpetic spot on the*

---

*v. "Senega in Paralysis of the Superior Rectus." H. D. Schenck, M. D., *Jour. of Oph., Otol. and Lar.*, May, 1911, p. 170.

upper lid, scaly and peeling. Pustules on the (left) conjunctiva. Eyes inflamed, injected, with swelling and burning; smarting, pressive pains; lacrimation, which relieves. Whites of eyes become yellow.

Subjective.—Lids feel heavy, *inclined to close, as from paralysis. Pressure as from sand, < rubbing and pressing lids together. Soreness, roughness and burning in the eyes, from walking in cold wind;* < gas-light, and from reading. Heat and dryness of lid margins; with much itching. Eyes feel very sore as if bruised. Dragging feeling in the eyes. Eyes hot and dry. Pressure at night. Burning in the morning. Eyes feel like balls of fire, < left, which is injected. Eyes sore to touch. *Smart in right eye in evening,* with inclination to close against one's wish. Eyes tire on reading and writing. Candle light fatigues the eyes, when reading or writing, by causing a contractive sensation. Can not bear reflected light from bright objects; it is annoying.

Vision.—Vanishing of sight. Obscured as by a veil. Photopsies, fiery sparks, zig-zags. Flickering on looking into a light; sees a zig-zag circle of colors. Many black spots. During menstruation everything goes black and clouded, in evening, with great weakness which passes off when lying down.

Characteristics.—Torpidity, depression, principally of the portal hepatic and female sexual systems. *Yellow saddle across the nose, and upper part of cheeks; also yellow or dirty yellow-brown spots on face and skin. Painful all gone sensation in stomach and abdomen. Urinary sediment of urates. Bearing down as if the contents of the pelvis would issue through the vulva, hence must cross her limbs. Exhaustion and faintness, in the morning,* during the menses. $<$ *morning and evening with* $>$ *in middle of the day.* A very important remedy.

Clinical.—*Chronic ciliary blepharitis,* often with *small pustules on the ciliary border.* Tarsal tumors have been relieved. Acute catarrhal conjunctivitis, with *drawing sensation in external canthus;* also with mucopurulent discharge in the morning and great dryness in the evening. Follicular conjunctivitis; mixed with trachoma. *Vernal conjunctivitis, during summer only or* $<$ *in hot weather.* Trachoma, with or without pannus, especially in *females addicted to tea.* Sometimes phlyctenular conjunctivitis. Of great value for phlyctenular keratitis, particularly in females with uterine trouble; also parenchymatous keratitis. Cataract, when properly indicated, progress checked and vision improved.

SILICEA—Sil.

Silica. Silex. Rock Crystal. Pure Flint.
SiO_2.

Objective.—*Swelling of right lacrimal gland and sac.* Lacrimation. Nocturnal agglutination. Lids twitch. *Ulcer on left eye.* Redness around eyes then also of the whites with inflammation and lacrimation.

Subjective.—Pressure in upper lid with violent twitches like a splinter, and vanishing of "visual power." Tension in eyes and forehead, with bodily weakness. Eyes painful, as if too dry and full of sand, in the morning. Piercing stinging pain in left eye. Tearing and burning in eyes on pressing them together. Heat and smarting in the eyes.

Vision.—Indistinct, misty, with flickering. Blackness after headache. Letters run together, can't read or write; they appear pale. Black spots.

Characteristics.—*Very sensitive to cold; wants to be warmly wrapped, particularly about the head.* Long lasting ulceration or suppuration; ulcers > warm and < by cold applications; pus is thin and offensive, often mixed with blood and sometimes with little particles that look like cheese. *Small wounds heal with difficulty, and suppurate profusely.*

Clinical.—*Caries of the orbital bones*—the most frequently indicated remedy. Dacryocystitis and acute lacrimal fistula. Blepharitis. Tarsal tumors. *Corneal ulcer, crescentic,* sloughing, small round, perforating, or non-vascular, central. The pain, photophobia and lacrimation are not specially marked. Valuable in *hypopion.* Choroiditis. Iridochoroiditis. Cataract. Ciliary neuralgia, with *darting pains through the eyes and head upon exposure to any draft of air,* or just before a storm.

SPIGELIA—Spig.

Pink Root.

Objective.—Mydriasis. Lids lax and paralyzed, hang low and must be raised with the hand. Whites inflamed. Lacrimation.

Subjective.—Pain as if upper lid were hard or immovable. Fine cutting, like a knife, on margin of left lower lid. Striking pressure under both lids. Pain as if left orbit were pressed from above downward. Sharp, shooting, cutting pains, *radiating* from the eye. *Tearing pains in forehead toward the orbits. Burning pain in right forehead extending to the eye so that he could not turn it without pain. Eyes hurt on motion as if too large for their orbits. Constant sticking pain in right eyeball, also on moving it.*

Violent burrowing stitch in the middle of the eye and inner canthus that does not prevent vision but presses upper lid downward. *Intolerable pressive pain in the balls, < turning them; dizzy on trying to look with the eyes turned, so that he was obliged to turn the whole head.* Contractive burning pain in right eyeball. Itching stitch in right ball, that returned after rubbing. Pain in eyes, deep in the sockets.

Characteristics.—One of the great neuralgia remedies, specially of the fifth pair of nerves, and in neuralgic and rheumatic affections of the heart. Generally < in stormy weather. *Pains radiate.*

Clinical.—The chief remedy for *ciliary neuralgia.* Its chief indications are the character and intensity of the pains. *Iritis.* Glaucoma. Ptosis. Corneal ulcer. Sclerochoroiditis. Asthenopia and anæmia of the optic nerve from too much tea drinking.

SPONGIA—Spong.

Sponge.

Clinical.—In homœopathic ophthalmic therapeutics the only use for spongia has been in exophthalmic goiter; in the higher potencies it has been curative.

STANNUM METALLICUM—Stann.

Metallic Tin. Sn.

Objective.—*Pustular swelling on left inner canthus.* Lacrimation. Nocturnal agglutination.

Subjective.—Pressive pain in left inner canthus as from a stye. Itching in the inner canthus.

Vision.—When reading, vertigo with loss of sight.

Characteristics.—Nervous exhaustion. *Pains increase and decrease slowly.* Copious secretion from mucous membranes, bland mucopurulent, yellowish or yellowish-green. *Weakness, emptiness, of the chest.*

STAPHYSAGRIA—Staph.

Stavesacre.

Objective.—Mydriasis. Eyes sunken, surrounded by blue rings. Marginal blepharitis.

Subjective.—*Itching of the lid margins.* Pain as from a hard substance lying beneath the upper lid. Pressure in the upper lid all day, < closing the eye. Eyes dry; in morning on waking; in evening, with pressure.

Characteristics.—Bad effects of sexual excess or onanism. Antidotes chronic effects of mercury; of thuja.

Clinical.—Blepharitis; but most commonly *tarsal tumors,* in recurrent crops; *chalazion; little hard nodules,* from styes; redness, tearing, tensive pains, < evening. Blepharitis with madarosis and dry lid margins with little hard nodules. Syphilitic iritis.

SULPHUR—Sulph.

S.

Objective.—*Lacrimation in the morning, with burning;* followed by dryness. Swelling and pain in the lids with lacrimation. *Eyes dry in the room, lacrimation in the open air. Lids red and swollen in the morning.* Redness of lids and conjunctiva. Eruption of pimples on upper lid. Heaviness of eyes. *Morning agglutination; nocturnal. Redness of eyes during the day, violent itching in the evening. Inflammation of the eyes or lids, with swelling, redness of conjunctivas.* A white vesicle on the white of the eye close to the cornea. Purulent mucus in the eyes.

Subjective.—*Much itching in the brows* and tip of nose; *of the lids with burning. Dryness of inner surface of lids. Burning, dryness, smarting, itching, of the lid margins, < morning. Sandy.* Sticking and burning in outer canthi. Pricking in eyes causes one to scratch and rub them. Biting of eyes and lacrimation every evening. Eyeballs painful on moving them. Pressure in them on walking in the open air. Painful smarting. *Burning in the eyes, with or* without *redness. Burning and easy fatigue on reading. Burning with great sensitiveness to daylight. In afternoon burning, shooting beneath left lids as of sand.* Sensation of foreign body. *Pain as from dryness of the balls and a sensation as if they rubbed against the lids. Violent pains in left eye, as if rubbed against glass spiculæ; had to close the eyes five or six times involuntarily; this was followed by burning and tears. Severe cutting in right eye.* Shooting in left eye, prevents him from reading for several days; on trying to read, immediately violent *shooting pains* through middle of pupil deep into eye. *Stitches as with a knife in right eye. In evening aching in eyeballs, with weight and loss of vision. Photophobia. Great sensitiveness to sunlight.*

Vision.—*Dim, like a veil, for near and distant objects.* Dimness like a fog with the headache. Dim vision, both eyes, *with great sensitiveness to bright daylight. Flickering. Dark points and spots.* Muscæ volitantes. Objects seem more distant than they really are. Obscuration of vision while reading. Must cover eyes with hand, slightly press and rub them, in order to read.

Often a feeling of heaviness and aching in the eyeballs when reading or writing.

Characteristics.—*Worse after washing, bathing. Early morning* <. Sulphur won its laurels chiefly in chronic diseases, but it is none the less important in acute conditions or as an intercurrent remedy. It is especially useful for people subject to skin eruptions, or after such eruptions have been *suppressed* (even many years before) *by local treatment.* Sharp darting pains like pin pricks.

Clinical.—*Blepharitis,* particularly chronic, and in strumous children who are irritable, cross, by day and *at night restless and feverish. Eczema, of the lids, as of other localities.* Blenorrhea of the lacrimal sac, but not often indicated. *Catarrhal conjunctivitis, acute or chronic; sharp darting pains like pin pricks.* Trachoma, acute or chronic; often an intercurrent remedy. Ophthalmia neonatorum, chronic and relapsing cases. Sulphur is the remedy "par excellence" for *pustular inflammation* of the cornea or conjunctiva, and in *ulcers and abscesses of the cornea,* superficial, deep, perforating or sloughing, *with* or without *hypopion,* particularly if *indolent* with no photophobia or vascularity. *Pannus,* true pannus crassum, or herpetic. *Parenchymatous keratitis,* is often used to promote absorption after other remedies have checked the disease. Kerato-iritis. Scleritis, and if there be iritic or corneal complications. Sometimes in iritis, *idiopathic* or syphilitic, especially if chronic. Choroiditis; chorioretinitis. Retinitis from overstudy. *Vitreous opacities* from choroidal exudations or old hæmorrhages. Asthenopia, muscular and accommodative; has cured paresis of the rectus externus.

SYMPHYTUM OFFICINALIS—Symph.

Comfrey. Chocolate Root.

Clinical.—This "arnica of the bones" may be useful when the orbital bones or their periosteum are suffering from trauma; also in case of irritable stump after amputation. Irritability of bone at point of fracture, delayed union.

TEREBINTHINA—Tereb.

Turpentine.

Characteristics.—*Albuminous, scanty, high colored, smoky, urine, with dull pains or burning in the region of the kidneys, the pain may extend from the kidney down through the ureter.*

Clinical.—*Excessive pain in or over the eye,* from dull, grumbling, aching, beating, sore, to severe sharp, darting, as if it would almost drive the patient crazy—involves the ball and is < *over* and around the eyes, through to corresponding side of occiput, often following supra-orbital nerve, *always* < *night;* sometimes paroxysms are < 1 to 3 a. m. Corresponding side of face is flushed. Conjunctival injection variable (moderate or excessive); there may be chemosis, and even infiltration of orbital cellular tissue. *Intense pain* with rheumatic iritis, episcleritis, or *ciliary neuralgia.* Deep ciliary injection, swelling of lids, photophobia, lacrimation; contracted pupil dilates slowly, regularly, under atropin. Tension, more frequently diminished, is changeable within a short time; ball sensitive to touch.

THUJA OCCIDENTALIS—Thu.

Arbor Vitæ.

Objective.—Nocturnal agglutination. Pimple on lower lid margin. Stye, right eye. White of eye much inflamed.

Subjective.—Tearing pain in left brow, disappears after touch. Lids feel swollen and as if a foreign body were in the eye. Burning and stinging in edges of lids, evening, and in the eyes, with injection. Eyes feel dry; sandy. Pressure in the eyes. A painful stitch through center of left eye, commencing in center of brain.

Vision.—Dim, like a mist, and pressure in eyes as if swollen or would be pressed out of the head. Dim vision in the open air, like a veil, for near and distant objects, with confusion of the head for half an hour. Muscæ volitantes. Great flickering. Sees a luminous disc like a fire fly.

Characteristics.—The typical remedy for sycosis—the constitutional taint following gonorrhea. Its characteristic action is the formation (hence the cure) of warts, condylomata, polypi, of skin and mucous membranes.

Clinical.—To be thought of if there be any history of gonorrhea, hereditary, latent or chronic. *Tarsal* (and other) *tumors,* verucæ and small condylomata; it has prevented their return after excision and even has absorbed them sometimes if only given internally. Thuja is the most prominent remedy for *scleritis, episcleritis,* sclerochoroiditis anterioris and commencing scleral staphyloma. Is a great remedy for syphilitic iritis with *gumma.*

TITANIUM METALLICUM—Tit.

Ti.

"Vertical" hemianopsia.

TRILLIUM—Tril.

Wake Robin.

Eyeballs feel too large.

Vision blurred; everything looks bluish.

VERATRUM ALBUM—Ver. a.

White Hellebore.

Objective.—*Eyes surrounded by black rings; by blue rings, and looked dull. Distorted, protruding. Redness; lacrimation. Pupils contracted; then dilated.* Dryness of lids. Agglutination.

Subjective.—Lids dry, < after sleep, painful as if rubbed sore, are stiff. Feeling as if salt were under the upper lid.

Vision.—Double.

Characteristics.—Prostration with cold sweat, particularly on the forehead, cold skin, great thirst.

ZINCUM METALLICUM—Zinc.

Zn.

Objective.—Nocturnal agglutination at inner canthus, *with a pressing sore feeling.* Upper lid red and swollen toward inner canthus. Suppuration in inner canthus. *Inflammation, redness, right conjunctiva, < inner canthus. Frequent lacrimation,* scalding, < evening.

Subjective.—Left lid burns as if too dry. *Feeling of soreness in inner canthi.* Outer canthus sore, with biting pain. Pressure on margin of left lower lid near inner canthus. Painful pressure in right inner canthus, with redness of conjunctiva. Constant pressure in left eye, in evening. Biting in right inner canthus, > by rubbing. Sore painful biting in eyes, toward evening, < right. *Itching and sticking pain at inner canthi,* with clouded sight. Eyeball feels dry. Constant burning in eyes with feeling of dryness and pressure. Tears hot, scalding. Frequent tickling in right eye, as from dust. Violent itching of left eye. Much photophobia. *Pains < evening and night.*

Vision.—Dim. Green rings.

Characteristics.—Zinc depresses the nervous system. Brain fag. Most symptoms appear after dinner and toward evening. < from wine. Nervous restlessness, *fidgety feet.*

Clinical.—*Pterygium,* a number of cases have been cured by its internal administration. Conjunctivitis, and it has also removed persistent redness of the conjunctiva remaining after pustular keratitis, < toward evening and in cool air, with no discharge. Amblyopia, with *great pressure across the root of the nose.* Ptosis.

CHAPTER IV.

REPERTORY.

One should continually bear in mind that the proper use of a repertory is but to suggest which remedies might well be studied in the materia medica.

In the Clinical Index the remedies in the first alphabetical sequence are the most apt, other things being equal, to prove of value. As usual, italics and small capitals indicate remedies of respectively greater value than those in ordinary type. At times the indicated remedy may with advantage be used locally, several drops of the tincture in water—or even hypodermatically.

It may be well to consult other symptoms in the repertory similarly worded to those being studied.

The sign ᵕ signifies that the only authority for the remedy so marked is clinical experience.

CLINICAL INDEX.

Abscess of lid—Con.

Amblyopia (Amaurosis)—Alum., Ars., Bell., *Chin. s.,* Filix mas, Gels., Nux, Salic. ac., Tabac., Wood alcohol.

Anæmia. Retinal—*Agar.,* Calc. c., *China,* Chin. s., Fer., Phos., Puls.

Asthenopia. Accommodative—*Agar.*, *Arg. n.*, Con., *Gels.*, JAB., LIL., Op., Paris, Phos., *Physos.*, RUTA, Sulph.; Bell., Calc. c., Caust., Cimic., Croc., Mercurial., Nux m., Spig.

Asthenopia. Muscular—*Agar.*, ALUM., Calc. c., *Con.*, GELS., JAB., Kalm., Led., Lil., *Mercurial.*, NAT. M., *Nux*, ONOS., *Paris*, *Physos.*, Rad., *Rhod.*, *Rhus*, Ruta, SEN., Sep.

Astigmia—*Lil.*, Physos.

Blepharitis—Ant. cr., Apis, Ars., *Bell.*, Calc. c., Calc. i., EUPH., GRAPH., HEP., IOD., MERC., Nat. ars., Nat. m., *Puls.*, *Rhus*, *Sulph.*; Acon., Alum., Arg. n., Aur., Calc. pic., Caust., Cinnab., Kreos., Lyc., Merc. cor., Merc. nit., Merc. prot., Mez., Nux, Petr., Pic. ac., Sang., Sen., Sep., Staph., Tell., Thu.

Blepharitis marginalis—Bor., GRAPH., *Merc.*

Blepharospasm (Nictitatio)—AGAR., *Physos.*; Alum., Bell., Cic., Ign., Nux.

Cataract—In the early stages this has been checked and even cured by the indicated remedy. Calc. ph., CAUST., Con., *Iodof.*, NAPH., PHOS., Sec., Sep.; Arg. n., Bar. c., Chin. ars., Ign., Kali i., Kali m., Lach., *Lyc.*, Mag. c., Nat. m., Nit. ac., Nux, Puls., Sen., Sil., Sulph.

Chalazion—PLATANUS OCCIDENTALIS, STAPH., *Thu.*; Calc. c., Caust., Con., Hep., Puls., Zinc.

Chloropsia (Sees green)—Ars., Calc. c., Caust., Cycl., *Dig.*, *Phos.*

Choroiditis—*Aur.*, *Bell.*, BRY., *Dub.*, Fe. ph., GELS., *Hep.*, Kali i., Kali m., Kalm., MERC. COR., MERC., *Nux*, *Phos.*, *Phyto.*, *Prun.*, RHUS; Acon., Ars., Crotal., Iod., Jab., Lach., Puls., Ruta, Sil., Sulph., Ver. v.

Chromatopsia (Sees colors)—BELL., *Bry.*, *Cina*, Cycl., *Dig.*, Mag. ph., *Phos.*, *Sant.*, Stram., Tril.

Commotio retinæ—ARN., HYPER.; Apis, Gels.

Conjunctivitis—Acet. ac., ACON., Alum., Ant. cr., *Apis*, ARG. N., Ars., Aur., Bar. i., BELL., Calc. c., Calc. i., Calc. hy., Calc. s., Caust., *Cepa*, Cham., Cinnab., Clem., Con., Crot. tig., Dub., EUPH., *Fe. ph.*, *Graph.*, *Hep.*, Ipec., Kali b., Kali i., Kreos., Lach., *Merc.*, Merc. cor., Merc. dulc., *Merc. nit.*, Merc. prec. rub., Merc. prot., *Nat. m.*, Nit. ac., Nux, Phyto., PULS., Rad., RHUS, Sang., Sep., Sulph., Tereb., Thu., Zinc.

Croupous—Acet. ac.

and Keratitis. Phlyctenular (See Phlyctenular).

Pustular. (See Pustular.)

Cyclophoria—Sen.°

Cyanopsia (Sees blue)—Kali c., Tril.; Aur., Lach., Stram., Agar.

Dacryoadenitis—Acon., Apis, *Hep.*, Iod., Rhus, Sil.

Day-blindness (see Hemeralopia).

Descemet's membrane, Deposits on ("Des-

Arn., Ars., Aur., Cham., Con., Crot. tig., Ham., Kali i., Macrotin, Merc., Sulph.

Hemeralopia (Day-blindness. Gk. ἡμερα, *hemera,* day, αλαος, *alaos,* blind, οψ, *ops.* eye) —Both., *Phos.,* Stram.

Hemianopsia—Calc. c., Calc. s., Caust., Plumb., Sep., *Tit.*

Horizontal (Dividing line)—Sep., *Tit.*

Upper half lost—Arn., Ars., AUR., *Dig.,* GELS.

Lower half lost—Aur.

Lateral (Vertical dividing line)—Calc. c., Morph., Mur. ac., Nat. m., Plumb.

Left—Cic.

Right—Cocc. ind., *Lith. c.,* LYC.

Herpes zoster ophthalmicus — CROT. TIG., RAN. B., Rhus; Ars., Canth., Graph., Merc., Puls.

Heterophoria (see Muscular asthenopia).

Iridochoroiditis—Apis, Ars. Asa., Aur., *Bell., Bry.,* GELS., *Hep.,* Kali i., *Merc. cor.,* Merc. prot., Prun., Sil., Sulph., Thu.

Iritis—Acon., Arn., Ars., Asa., Aur., BELL., BRY., Calc. hy., Ced., China, Chin. m., Cinnab., Clem., Con., Euph., Gels., Ham., Hep., Kali b., Kali i., Merc., MERC. COR., Merc. dulc., Merc. prot., Nat. sal., Nux, Nit. ac., Petr., Rhus, SPIG., Sulph., Tereb., Thu.

Keratitis (see Conjunctivitis).

Parenchymatous—Apis, Ars., AUR., Bar. i., Calc. ph., *Can. sat.*, Fe. ph., Hep., Kali i., KALI M., Merc., Sep., SULPH., or other preparations of calc., kali and merc.

Phlyctenular (see Phlyctenular).

Pustular (see Pustular).

Keratoconus—The progress of conical cornea has been checked with the indicated homœopathic remedy, which however does not lessen the conicity—Calc. i., Puls.

Lacrimal fistula (see Fistula lacrimalis).

Lupus—Apis, Hydrocot., Iodof., Phyto., Radium, Thu.

Madarosis—Bor.

Muscular insufficiency—*Con.*, NAT. M., *Physos.*, *Rhod.*, Ruta. See Asthenopia, Muscular.

Nerve. Optic (see Optic nerve).

Neuralgia. Ciliary and Ocular—Acon., Arn., Ars., Amyl, *Asa.*, Bad., *Bell.*, China, Chin. m., Cimic., CINNAB., *Coloc.*, Croc., *Hyper.*, Ign., Ipec., Kali ph., *Mag. ph.*, Mez., Nat. m., Nat. sal., *Plant.*, Phyto., PRUN., Rad., Sang., Sil., SPIG., Tereb., Thu.

Infraorbital—Arg. n., Ars., Bell., Kalm.

Supraorbital—*Asa.*, CED., Chel., China, Chin. s., CINNAB., Ign., Kalm., *Mag. ph.*, Nat. m., Nux, Sep.

Neuritis. Retrobulbor—Ars., *Nux,* Tereb.; Fe. ph., Kali ph. This has been caused by the following, any one of which may, too, be of remedial value: Amyl (wood) alcohol, Atoxyl., Can. ind., Carbon bisulphid, Dinitrobenzol, Iodoform, Nitrobenzol, Lead, Stramonium, Tobacco.

Nyctalopia (Night-blindness, from Gk. *νυξ, nux,* night, αλαος, *alaos,* blind, οψ *ops,* eye) *China,* LYC., Nit. ac., Ran. b.

Nystagmus—AGAR., *Bell.,* Hyos., Ign., Mag. ph., Stram.; Jab., Physos., Nux.

Oculomotor paralysis—*Acon.,* CAUST., Gels., *Rhus;* Arn., Chel., Cup. acet., Kali i., Merc. prot., Nux, Paris, Phos., Sen., Spig.; or Alum., Aur., Con.

Optic Nerve, Atrophy of—*Arg. n.,* Ars., NUX, *Phos.,* PLUMB., Strych. ph., Ver. v., Zinc ph.
Inflammation of (see Retinitis).

Orbital cellulitis—Acon., Apis, HEP., IOD., Lach., Merc., PHYTO., RHUS, SIL.; Ars., Bell., Bry., Kali i., Sulph.
periostitis, caries, necrosis—Aur., Calc. hy., Kali i., Merc., SIL.; Asa., Calc. c., *Fl. ac., Hecla lava,* Lyc., Mez., Nit. ac., Petr., Phos., Sulph., Symph.

Pannus—AUR., Hep., Merc., Rhus, Sulph.; Alum., Can. sat., Kali b., Merc. bin., Sil.

Panophthalmitis—RHUS; Apis, Ars., HEP., *Iod.*, *Phyto.*; Acon., Asa., Bell., Merc., Sil., Sulph.

Paralysis of accommodation—Arg. n., BELL., Caust., *Dub.*, GELS.

of extrinsic ocular muscles—Acon., *Alum.*, CAUST., *Con.*, GELS., Kali i., Nat. m., SEN., Rhus; may be Arn., Aur., Chel., Cup. acet., Hyos., Merc. prot., Nux, Paris, Phos., Spig., Sulph.

Phlyctenular conjunctivitis and keratitis—*Ant. cr.*, *Ant. t.*, Apis, Ars., Aur., Bar. c., Bar. i., Calc. c., Calc. hy., Calc. i., Calc. pic., Calc. s., Cham., Con., Crot. tig., Euph., Graph., *Hep.*, *Ipec.*, Kali b., Lach., Merc., Merc. cor., Merc. dulc., *Merc. nit.*, Merc. prot., *Nat. m.*, Nux, Puls., RAN. B., Rhus, *Sep.*, Sulph., Thu.

Pterygium—Calc. c., Chimaph., ZINC.; Arg. n., Ars., Calc. c., Can. ind., Rat., Spig., Sulph.

Ptosis—*Acon.*, *Alum.*, CAUST., Con., GELS., Kalm., Rhus; Con., Euph., Led., Rad., Spig., Stan.

Pustular conjunctivitis and keratitis—*Ant. cr.*, Ars., Calc. c., *Calc. i.*, Calc. s., Can. sat., Con., Crot. tig., Graph., *Hep.*, Ipec., Kali b., *Merc.*, Puls., Rhus, Sep., SULPH., Tell.

Retinal hyperesthesia—*Bell.*, CON., IGN., Lact., ac., Macrotin, *Merc.*, Nat. m., Nux; Acon., Ant. t., Ars., China, Gels., Hep., Hyos., Puls., Rhus, Sep., Sulph.

Retinitis, Neuroretinitis and Hyperæmia—BELL., DUB., GELS., PHOS.; Acon., Ars., Aur., Bry., Cact., Chin. s., Con., Fe. ph., Kali i., Kali m., Lach., Merc., Naph., Nux, Puls., Sec., Spig., Sulph., Ver. v.

albuminurica—Apis, Ars., KALM., MERC. COR.; Gels., Hep., Kali i., Plumb., Phos.

hæmorrhagic—Arn., BELL., CROTAL., DUB., LACH., MERC. COR., PHOS.

pigmentosa—Lyc., Nux, Phos.

punctata albescens—Naph.

syphilitic—*Asa., Aur., Kali i.,* MERC. COR. or sol., Nit. ac.

Scleritis (see episcleritis).

Scleroticochoroiditis posterioris—Bell., Dub., Phos., Prun., Spig., Thu.; Carbo v., Croc., Jab., Lyc., Kali i., Kalm., Merc., Physos., Ruta, Sep., Sulph.

Scrofulous ophthalmia—Ant. cr., Ant. t., Ars., Ars. iod., Aur., Bad., Bar. c., Bar. i., Calc. c., Can. sat., Cham., Chin. ars., Graph., Hep., Iod., Merc. cor., Merc. dulc., Merc. nit., Nit. ac., Puls.

Spasm of the orbicularis—Agar., Chin. s., Os., Physos.; Ars., Calc., Con., Hep., Merc. cor., Rhus.

of the ciliary muscle—AGAR., Cic., Eserin, *Jab.*, PHYSOS., LIL. TIG., Nux.

Strabismus—Agar., Alum., Arn., *Bell.*, Chel.,

Cic., CINA, Cupr., Cycl., Eserin, GELS., Hell., *Hyos.*, Jab., Kali i., Mag. ph., Nux, SEN., Spig., Stram.

Sympathetic ophthalmia—Bell., Bry., Kali i., Merc., Rhus, Sil.

Syphilis of the eye—Ars., Asa., Aur., Cinnab., Hep., Kali i., MERC., MERC. PROT., MERC. COR., *Nit. ac.*, Staph., Thu.

Tenonitis—Bry., KALM., Kali i., Puls., Rhus.

Trachoma—Alum., *Arg. n.*, *Aur.*, Kali b., Merc., *Nat. m.*, Nux, Puls., Rhus, Sulph.; Acon., Alumen, Ars., Bell., Calc. c., Chin. m., Cup., Euph., Sep., Thu.

Trichiasis—Bor.

Ulcus corneæ—Arg. n., ARS., *Aur.*, Bell., *Calc. c.*, CALC. HY., *Calc. i.*, Cham., Chin. ars., Chin. m., *Cinnab.*, CON., *Graph.*, HEP., Ipec., KALI B., Lach., *Merc. cor.*, *Merc. dulc.*, MERC. NIT., Merc. prec. rub., *Merc. prot.*, Nat. m., Nux, Puls., RHUS, Sil., Spig., *Sulph.*, Thu.; Alum., Apis, Arn., Asa., Bar. c., Bar. i., Can. sat., Crot. tig., Dub., Ign., Kali c., Kali i., Kali m., Kreos., Merc. bin., Nat. c., Nit. ac., Petr., Sang., Sec., Sen., Sep.

Uveitis—AUR., BRY., GELS., KALI B., RHUS, Arn., Hep., Kali i., Merc., Sil.

Wounds—ACON., in the beginning; ARN., bruises, ecchymosis and (later) for absorption;

CALEND., cuts and raw surfaces; HYPER. ("the arnica of the nerves") for pain after operation or trauma; Cepa, pain after operation, specially in cataract extraction; Led., punctures or insect stings; Symph., bruised periosteum and bone, delayed osseous union (The "arnica of the bones").

OBJECTIVE SYMPTOMS.

Aqueous cloudy—Crotal.
Blinking—*Agar.*, *Sulph.*
Blood, To absorb—Arn., Crotal., Ham., Lach.
  exudes from the eye—Crotal.
Blue around the eye (see Dark).
Brow twitches—AGAR., Caust., Cina.
Canthi crack or bleed—GRAPH.
  External, sore—Ant. cr., *Bor.*, GRAPH., Hep.
  Inner—Acon., Bor., ZINC.
Caries of the orbital bones—SIL.
Caruncle inflamed—Arg. n.
Cellulitis (see Orbit).
Chemosis—Acon., APIS, *Cham.*, Kali i., Kali m., RHUS, Tereb.
Choked disc—Bell., Dub., Merc., Phos., Plumb.; Apis, Hell.
Conjunctiva injected (congested) — ACON.,

Alum., Apis, Bar. c., BELL., Cham., Chloral, Crot. tig., Glon., Hyos., Ipec., Kali b., Mercurial., Mez., Natr. ars., Nux, Petr., Sep., Stram., Sulph., Thu.
dirty red—Mez.
Palpebral, like velvet—ARG. N.
Cornea hazy—Calc. s., Coccul., Gels., Kali b., Kali i., *Kali m.*, *Sulph.*
inflamed (see Clinical Index).
injected—*Can. sat.*, Ipec.
Corneal abscess—*Calc. hy.*, Fe. ph., HEP., Merc., *Rhus*, Sil., *Sulph.*
opacities—Aur., Bar. c., *Calc. c.*, *Calc. i.*, Can. sat., Hep., Kali b., Kali m., Nat. s., Sil., *Sulph.*
ulcer. Asthenic—CALC. HY.
Central—Sil.
Crescentic—Calc. hy., *Sil.*
Deep—Calc. c., Calc. hy., Graph., Hep., Kali b., Merc. cor., Merc. dulc., Merc. nit., Sulph.
Indolent—KALI B., Kali c., Kali m., Sulph.
Malarial—Ced., Chin. m.
Marginal—*Merc. prot.*
Nonvascular—*Con.*, KALI B., Puls., Sil., Sulph.
Perforating—Kali b., Nit. ac., Sil., Sulph.
Round—Kali c., Sil.

Serpigenous—*Merc. prot.*
Sloughing—Calc. hy., HEP., Sil., Sulph.; Arg. n., Calc. c.
Small round—Sil., Sulph.
Superficial—CON., Graph., *Ipec.*, Kali m., Lach., Merc., *Merc. prot.*, Nat. c.; Ars., Bar. c., Bell., Calc. i., Cham., Cimic., Crot. tig., Cund., Euph., Merc. cor., Merc. dulc., *Merc. nit.*, Nat. m., Nux, Puls., Rhus, Spig., Thu.
Vascular—Apis, Ars., Aur. met., Can. sat., Fe. ph., Hep., *Ipec.*, Kali m., *Merc.*, Merc. cor., Sulph.
with yellowish base—Kali b., Kali m.

Dark rings around the eyes—Acet. ac., *Cina, Crotal.*, Kali b., Nux m., Phos., Staph., *Sec., Ver. a.*

Discharge acrid thick—EUPH.
thin—Ars., Graph., *Merc.*
bland thick—ARG. N., *Calc. s.*, *Hep.*, PULS., Stan.
clear mucus—Nat. m., Stan.
mucopurulent—Arg. n., Cham., Graph., Lyc., Sep., Stan., Sulph.
profuse on separating the lids—ARG. N., Calc. s., Fer., HEP., Ipec., RHUS.
pus—*Calc. s.*, HEP., Puls., Rhus, SIL.
stringy—Kali m.
thin and offensive—*Sil.*

yellow—Arg. n., CALC. S., *Hep.*, Puls., Stan.
stringy—KALI B.
Ecchymosis—ARN., *Crotal.*, *Ham.*, *Lach.*
Epiphora—Petr.
Esophoria—Bell., Sulph.
Exophoria—NAT. M., Physos., Rhod., Ruta.
Eyes bright—BELL., Clem., *Hyos.*
congested during headache—Bell., Cimic.
dry—ACON., Bar. c., BELL., Clem., *Mercurial.*, Pic. ac., Puls., Sang., Sep., Sulph.
dull—Fer., Onos., Ver. a.
fixed—*Sec.*
inflamed—ACON., Apis, BELL., Caust., Colch., Fe. ph., Iod., Mez., RHUS, Sep., Spig., Thu.
moving constantly—Bell.
protrude—Aur. met., *Bell.*, Glon., Iod., Ver. a.
roll—Hyos.
red—ACON., Aur., BELL., Calc. c., Chloral, Cinnab., Clem., Crotal., Fer., Fe. ph., Gels., Graph., Ham., HEP., Hyos., Ipec., Kali b., Kali c., *Merc.*, *Nat. m.*, Op., Rhus, Sang., Sec., Sil., *Sulph.*, Thu., Ver. a.
staring—Bell., Cic., Glon., Hyos., Sec., *Stram.*
sunken, with dark rings—Acet. ac., Phos., *Sec.*, Staph., Ver. a.
twitches in the—AGAR., PHYSOS.
wild—Hyos., Sec., *Stram.*
yellow—CHELID., China, Con., *Crotal.*, Iod., Pic. ac., *Plumb.*, Sep.

Fundus anæmic—Chin. s.
congested—BELL., DUB., Gels., Onos., Os.
veins large and tortuous—Dub., Os.
Hæmorrhage. Intraocular—Arn., *Crotal.*, Ham., *Lach.*, *Led.*
Retinal—Crotal., Lach., Merc. cor., Phos.
Hypopion—Calc. hy., Calc. s., Graph., HEP., Merc., Sil., SULPH.
Iris congested—Gels.
Lacrimal gland swollen—*Sil.*
Lacrimal sac swollen, inflamed—IOD., Petr., PULS., Rhus, Sep., Sil., Stan., Staph.
Lacrimation (bland)—Acet. ac., Arg. n., Bell., Cann. sat., Caust., CEPA, Cham., Chel., China, Chin. ars., Chin. s., Colch., Con., Crotal., Crot. tig., Fer., Graph., Hep., Ign., Ipec., Kali c., Kali i., Lil., Mag. ph., Mercurial., Nat. s., Nit. ac., Nux, Os., Petr., Physos., Phyto., Puls., Rhus, Ruta, Sang., *Sep.*, Sil., Spig., Stan., *Sulph.*, Tereb., Ver. a., Zinc.
acrid—*Ars.*, Calc. c., EUPH., Kreos., Led., *Lyc.*, *Merc.*, *Merc. cor.*, Mez., Nat. m.
hot (burning)—Apis, ARS., *Canth.*, Cedr. Chin. ars., Euph., *Kreos.*, Merc., Nat. ars., Rhus, Sen., *Sulph.*, Zinc.
Lids agglutinated—Ant. cr., Aur., Phyto., Sep., Sec.
blink—*Agar.*, SULPH.
bluish—Bad., PHYTO.

close involuntarily—Nat. c., Sep.
closed forcibly, spasmodically—Hep., Merc., Nat. m.
droop—*Alum.*, Apis, Bell., CAUST., Con., *Gels.*, Nat. c., Nit. ac., Nux m., Op., Phos., *Pic. ac.*, Rhus, Sep., Spig., Sulph.
dry, inner surface—*Sulph.*
edematous—Acet. ac., APIS, *Ars.*, KALI C., Kali i., Phos., *Phyto.*, RHUS.
edges inflamed—Acon., GRAPH., Nux, Staph.
 red—Ant. cr., Bell., Chel., *Euph.*, GRAPH., Kali b., Lil., Nat. ars., *Nat. m.*, *Petr.*, *Puls.*, Staph.
 sore—Ant. cr., Ars., Bad., EUPH., *Lyc.*, *Merc.*
inflamed—Acon., Apis, Ant. cr., *Arg. n.*, Ars., Bad., Bar. c., *Bell.*, Calc. c., Coccul., *Euph.*, *Hep.*, IOD., *Lyc.*, *Merc.*, Petr., PHYTO., PULS., RHUS, Sulph.
morning agglutination—Alum., Ant. cr., Aur., Bry., Calc. c., Caust., Dig., Dub., Hep., Kali b., *Lyc.*, Merc., Nat. ars., Nat. m., Nat. s., Pic. ac., *Puls.*, *Rhus*, *Sulph.*
moving constantly—Colch.
nocturnal agglutination—Bor., Sil., Stan., *Sulph.*, Thu., Zinc.
puffy—APIS, ARS., Bell., Bry., Crot. tig., Cycl., Dub., Iod., KALI C., Nat. ars., RHUS.
red—*Hep.*, Ipec.

and swollen—Aur., Calc. c., Dig., *Euph.*, IOD., PHYTO., PULS., *Rhus*, *Sulph.*
swollen—Cham., Fer., Ham., *Hep.*, Lyc., *Merc.*, Nit. ac., *Phyto.*, Sulph.
twitch—AGAR., Alum., *Bell.*, Calc. c., Chel., *Cic.*, Croc., *Jab.*, Mag. ph., Mercurial., *Mez.*, *Nux*, Paris, *Physos.*, Sil.
wink constantly—Ign.
frequently—Caust., Croc., *Euph.*, Nux, Sulph.

Meibomian glands hardened—Bad.
secretion increased—Nat. m.

Mydriasis—BELL., Calc. c., *Caust.*, Chin. s., Cimic., Cina, Con., Croc., Dig., DUB., *Gels.*, Glon., Led., Mercurial., Rhod., Sang., Spig., Staph., *Stram;* Arn., Apis, Hyos., Nux, Plumb.

Myosis—Agar., Cic., Clem., Coccul., Ipec. *Jab.*, Mag. ph., Merc., OP., PHOS., PHYSOS.

Nystagmus—Gels., Mag. ph.

Onyx—Merc., Rhus.

Optic disc anæmic—China, Chin. s., Chloral.
brilliant points—Naph.
congested—BELL., DUB., Onos., Plumb.
inflamed—BELL., Plumb.

Orbital cellular tissue infiltration—APIS, Fe. ph., Nat. ars., Tereb.

Puffiness over the eyes—KALI C., Nat. ars., Phos.
under the eyes—ARS., Phos.

Pupillary action, Consensual, impaired—Bell.

Pupil immobile—Bad., BELL., Cic., Hyos.
sluggish—*Bell.*, Con., Gels.; Acon., Kali b.
Retina anæmic—China, Chin. s., Fer.
congested—BELL., Bry., Crotal., DUB., Glon., Phos., Sang.
hazy—*Bell.*, Gels., Merc. cor.
white punctate spots in—Naph.
Retinal arteries enlarged—BELL., *Dub.*
small—Amyl, Dub.
veins enlarged—Amyl, Bell.
Sclera red (see Clinical Index).
Tension diminished—Tereb.
increased—*Bell.*, Gels., *Os.*
Vitreous hazy—*Aur.*, Gels., *Kali i.*, Kali n., Lyc., Phos., Sulph.
opacities—Arg. n., Arn., AUR., Bry., CROTAL., Gels., HAM., Jab., KALI I., Kalm., Lach., Led., *Lyc.*, Merc., Merc. prot., Nat. m., Phos., Prun., *Sen.*, Sil., Sulph.
Winks constantly—Ign.
frequently—Caust., Croc., *Euph.*, Nux, Sulph.
Yellowness about eyes with red cheeks—Nit. ac.
across eyes and face—SEP.

SUBJECTIVE SYMPTOMS.

Ache (see Eyes).
Aching (see Pain).
Air, Eyes sensitive to—ACON., Caust., Colch., Hep., Kali b., Sep., Sil., Sulph.

Brow aches—Nat. ars.
  Boring over—Asa.
  Pain and heaviness over—*Aloe,* Lith. c.
  Pressure in—Arn.
    over—*Ruta.*
  Tearing in—Arn., Thu.
Canthi, as if adhere—Alum., Zinc.
  itch—Alum., Arg. n., Lyc.
  soreness in—Cham., Ran. b., *Zinc.*
Canthus, Inner, biting—Puls., Zinc.
    burning—Aur., Calc. c., Caust., Cinnab. Petr.
    drawing—Aur., Cinnab.
    dryness—Nux.
    itching—Aur., Calc. c., Caust., Cinnab. Nat. m., Ruta, Stan., *Zinc.*
    pressive pain—Puls., Stan.
    pressure—Petr., *Zinc.*
    smarts—Con., Nux.
    soreness—Puls., *Zinc.*
    sticking pain—*Spig.*
    stitches—Aur., Calc. c., Cinnab., *Zinc.*
  Outer, biting—Zinc.
    burning pain—Kali c., Sulph.
    drawing—Sep.
    sore feeling—Ant. cr., Kali c.
    the worse—Nux.
Contraction in the eyes—PHYSOS., Sep.

Drawing and fatigue in the extraocular muscles —Onos., Physos.

Excessive, Pains are—CHAM., Como., *Prun.*, SPIG., *Tereb.*

Eyes (see Pain).

ache—*Acon.*, Bell., Carbo v., CIMIC., Como., Fer., Hep., Lach., Phos., Rad., RUTA, *Sulph.*

burn—*Acon.*, *Agar.*, Alum., Arg. n., Arn., *Ars.*, Asa., Bry., Carbo v., Caust., Cham., China, Con., Croc., Crotal., Cycl., Euph., Fer., Fe. ph., Ign., *Jab.*, Kali b., Kali c., Lil., Lyc., Mercurial., Merc., Nat. m., Nat. s., Nit. ac., Op., Os., Phos, Puls., *Ruta*, *Sep.*, Sil., *Sulph.*, Thu., Zinc.

feel bursting—PRUN.

compressed—Nat. m.

constricted—Chloral.

drawn backward—Bry., Crot. tig., PARIS.

dry—ACON., ALUM., Ars., Asa., *Caust.*, Cycl., Dub., Fe. ph., Graph., Ign., Lith. c., *Lyc.*, Mercurial., *Mez.*, Nat. ars., Nat. m., *Nux m.*, Op., Pic. ac., Rad., Rhod., Sang., Sen., *Sep.*, Sil., Staph., Thu., Zinc.

enlarged—Acon., Ars., Bell., COMO., Glon., Mercurial., *Nat. m.*, Op., Paris, *Phyto.*, Rhus, Sen., Spig., Tril.

fall out when stooping—Coloc.

forced out—Ham., Led., Mercurial., Thu.
full—Nux m.
heavy—*Aloe,* Alum., Arn., Bell., *Como.,* Nat. c., *Onos.,* Paris, Physos.
open wide—Onos.
protruding—Acon., *Como.,* Fer., Glon., Paris, Spong.
pushed into the orbit—Acon.
sandy—(see Sand).
smaller—Bry.
sore—*Bry.,* Cinnab., Croc., Eup. perf., Fe. ph., Gels., Ham., Hep., Onos., Physos., Ran. b., *Rhus,* Sang., *Sep.,* Zinc.
stiff—*Bry.,* Lach., Onos., Phos., Rhus.
weak (tired)—Agar., Aur. met., Bar. c., Bell., Carbo v., Chloral., China, *Con.,* Dub., Jab., Lach., Lil., Nat. ars., Nat. s., Op., Physos., Sen.

itch—Acon., AGAR., Ant. cr., Apis, Arg. n., Arn., Bar. c., Bell., Calc. c., Caust., *Euph.,* Kali b., Lyc., Mez., Nat. m., Nat. s., Petr., RHUS, Ruta, Zinc.

pain (see Pain).

sensitive to touch—Agar., Aur., Bell., Cham., Hep., Lach., Sep.

smart—Acon., Bell., Clem., Croc., Graph., Hep., *Jab.,* Kali b., Kali c., Lil., Mez., Nat. ars., Nat. m., Nit. ac., Physos., Phyto., Ran. b., Sen., *Sep.,* Sil.

tire easily—Apis, Caust., JAB., Nat. ars., *Nat. m., Onos.,* Petr., Phos., Physos., RUTA, Sep., *Sulph.*

Foreign body, Sensation of a, in the eye—Ign., Nat. m., Phyto., Pic. ac., Puls., Rhus, *Sulph.,* Thu.

Heat in the eyes—*Acon.,* Arg. n., Ars., Aur., Cham., China, Clem., Dub., Graph., *Jab.,* Kali b., Lil., Merc., Mez., Nat. m., Phos., Puls., Rhod., *Ruta,* Sil.

in the lids—Lil., Phyto.

Involuntarily closes the eyes—*Sulph.*

Jerks in the eyeball—Agar., Lach., PHYSOS.

Lid margin feels sore—Ars., EUPH., *Graph.,* Nat m., Nux, Phyto., *Sulph.*

Upper, pressed down by a sticking pain—*Spig.*

Lids burn—*Ars.,* Aur., Con., *Euph.,* Graph., Led., Nat. m., Nat. s., *Puls.,* Ran. b., *Sulph.,* Thu.

drawing in—Agar., Bry.

feel dry—Euph., Fe. ph., Graph., Lyc., Petr., Puls., Sep., Sulph., Zinc., Ver. a.

heavy—*Alum.,* Asa., Bry., CAUST., Cinnab., Con., *Gels., Graph., Mercurial.,* Nat. ars., Nat. s., Nux m., Onos., Physos., Sep., Staph.

raw—Phyto.

stiff—Nux m.

itch—Caust., *Euph.*, Mez., Petr., *Puls.*, Ruta, Sep., *Staph.*, SULPH.

Nausea with aching in orbit—Physos.

on looking at moving objects—JAB.

on near vision—JAB., Physos.

Open. Disposition to press the eyes—Led., Sulph.

Eyes feel as if wide—Onos.

Opening eyes is difficult—Lyc., Mercurial., Nat. ars., Nat. c., Nit. ac., Nux m.

Orbit. Aching in—Sen.

edge feels bruised—Aur.

Pain around—CINNAB., Kali b.

Expansion in—Onos.

Pain in depths of—*Aloe*, Arg. n., Bry., Gels., Led., Mag. ph., Nat. ars., Onos., Physos., Phyto., Spig.

—, Dull—Nuph., Onos.

—, Sharp—Cham., Kali c., Os., *Spig.*

Pressure in—Cham., China, Clem., Led., Ruta, Spig.

Weight in—Nuph.

Pain. Aching—Bad., Bell., Bry., Chel., Coloc., *Como.*, Gels., Nat. ars., Phos., Physos., Phyto., *Ruta.*

Biting—Agar., *Arg. n.*, Caust., Clem., Croc., Euph., Graph., Kali c., Merc., Mez., Nit. ac., Puls., Rhus, Zinc.

Bruised—Acon., ARN., Aur., Coccul., Gels., Hep., Ruta, Sep.

Boring—Arg. n., *Asa.,* Coloc.
Burning—Ars., Asa., Aur., Calc. c., Caust., Clem., Coloc., Fer., Graph., Kali c., Os., Ran. b., Ruta, Spig.
Bursting—Como., *Prun.*
Crawling—China.
Crushed. As if—Prun.
Cutting—Sulph.
Darting—*Sil.*
Drawing—Aur., Gels., Lach., Paris, *Physos.,* Sen., Sep., Spig.
Dull—Nuph., Onos., Phos., Physos., Phyto., Sen.
Excessive—*Como., Cham., Prun., Spig., Tereb.*
Heavy—Onos.
Intermittent—Bad., *Bry.,* Chin. m.
extends inward—Aur.
like lightning—*Prun.*
extends outward—Asa.
Periodic—Cedron, Chin. s., Prun., Rhod.
Pressive—Aur., Bell., *Bry.,* Caust., Chel., Coccul., Con., Glon., Hep., Lyc., Mez., Nux, Puls., Ran. b., Sil., *Spig.*
Pricking—Sulph.
quickly comes and goes—Bell., Ced., Fer., *Prun., Spig.*
Radiating—Cedron., Coloc., Spig.
Raw—Iod., Phyto.

screwing—COLOC.

Shooting—Acon., Bell., *Ced.*, Hep., Kali b., Kali c., Lach., Lil., *Prun.*, Rad., SPIG., Sulph.

Sharp, stitching—Agar, Apis., Ars., ATROP., Aur., *Bell.*, Calc. c., Ced., Cham., Chel., Chin. s., Coloc., Dub., Fer., KALI C., Lach., Lil., Lyc., Nat. c., Nat. m., *Nit. ac.*, Os., Paris, Petr., Physos., Prun., Sang., SPIG., SULPH., Thu., *Zinc.*

Smarting—Iod., Phyto.

like splinters—NIT. AC., Sulph.

Sticking—Petr., Physos., Pic. ac., *Spig.*, *Sulph.*, Zinc.

Stinging—*Apis, Caust.*, Crot. tig., Fer., Nat. c., Sil.

Tearing—Arn., Chel., Coccul., Colch., Ipec., Sil., *Spig.*, Thu.

Throbbing—Ars., Asa, BELL., *Hep.*

Twisting—COLOC., Mag. ph., Physos.

Unbearable—CHAM.

Violent—Coloc., COMO., Mag. ph., *Prun.*, Ran. b., SPIG., Tereb.

above the eye (see Supraorbital).

around the eye—Asa, Coloc., Cinnab.

around edge of orbit—CINNAB., *Kali b.*

behind the eye—Arg. n., Bad., BELL., Gels., Led., Physos.

in the eye—*Asa.*, Bad., BELL., *Bry.*, Calc. c.,

Ced., Clem., Coccul., Colch., COMO., Croc., Crot. tig., *Dub.*, Fe. ph., *Glon.*, *Hep.*, Ipec., *Jab.*, Mercurial., Onos., Phos., PHYSOS., Phyto., PRUN., Ran. b., Rhus, Sang., Spig., Sulph., *Tereb.*°

into the eye down from the head—Aur. met., Chloral., Ign., Lach., *Spig.*

from middle of brain—Thu.

from above eye to occiput—CIMIC., Physos., Prun., Tereb.

eye to occiput—Cimic., Gels., *Paris*, Physos., Prun.

to vertex—Cimic.

Photophobia—Acon., Alum., Ant. cr., *Arg. n.*, Arn., ARS., Aur., Bar. c., BELL., Bry., Calc. c., Can. sat., *Caust.*, *Cham.*, China, Chin. ars., Chin. s., Cic., Clem., CON., *Croc.*, Dig., Eup. perf., *Euph.*, Fer., Gels., Graph., *Hep.*, Ign., Ipec., Kali c. Lach., Lil., *Lyc.*, Mag. ph., Mercurial., MERC., Nat. ars., Nat. c., Nat. m., Nat. s., *Nit. ac.*, *Nux*, Physos., Phyto., *Sulph.*, Tereb., Zinc.

Pressure above the eyes—Crotal., Kali c., Merc., Nat m., *Ruta*, Spig.

around the eyes—*Phyto.*, Sen.

downward on the eyeball—Bry., Carbo v., Como.

in the brow—Arn., Ruta.

in the inner canthus—Petr., Zinc.
in the eyeball—Acon., Agar., Alum., *Bell.*, *Cycl.*, Lach., Sen.
in the eyes—Aur. met., Calc., *Caust.*, Cham., *China,* Coccul., Con., Croc., Hep., Kali b., Kali c., Sen., Sep., Staph., Sulph., THU., Zinc.
in the orbit—Cham., China, Clem., Led., Ruta, Spig.

Rub the eyes. Must—Mez., Sulph.

Sand. Feels as if there were, in the eyes—ACON., Ars., Aur., Calc. c., *Caust.*, *Fe. ph.*, *Fl. ac.*, *Hep.*, Ign., Lil., Lyc., *Nat. m.*, Op., Phyto., Pic. ac., Puls., Rhus, Sep., Sil., *Sulph.*, Thu., Ver. a.

Sleep. Eyes feel as if he had lost too much—Onos.

Splinters. Pains like—Hep., NIT. AC., *Sulph.*

Stiffness around the eyes—Kalm.

Supraorbital pain (or "over the eye")—Asa, Bry., CED., *Chel.*, Chin. s., *Cimic.*, Cina, *Crot. tig.*, *Dub.*, Fer., Gels., Glon., Ipec., Kali b., Lach., Lil., Mag. ph., Nat. ars., *Nat. m.*, Onos., Physos., *Prun.*, Sang., *Tereb.*, Thu.

Tension, sensation, in the eyes—*Aur.*, Ipec., Kali c., Onos., Physos.

Torn out of the head. Pain as if eyes—Coccul.

Wind blowing in the eye. A feeling of—FL. AC., Mez.

VISION.

Accommodation sluggish—*Con.*, Nat. m.
weak—Arg. n., *Bell.*, Caust., DUB., JAB., Nat. m.

All colors appeared white—Con.

Approximation of near and far points—*Jab.*

Astigmia. Spasmodic—LIL., PHYSOS.

Blindness—Bell.

Blue (see Cyanopsia).

Bluish, Objects look—Tril.

Chloropsia (sees green)—*Dig.*, Kali c., Stram., Zinc.; Ars., Calc. c., Caust., Cycl., Phos.

Chromopsia (see Chromatopsia in Clinical Index).

Ciliary spasm—Cic., JAB., LIL., Physos.

Colors (see Chromopsia).

Confusion on rising—China.

Coughing. Sees sparks after—Nuph.

Cyanopsia (see blue)—*Agar.*, Kali c., Stram., Tril.; Aur., Lach.

Day blindness (see Hemeralopia in Clinical Index).

Dazzled. Eyes feel—Sen.

Dilating pupils by shading them. Sees >—Phos., Sulph.

Diplopia—*Aur.*, Bell., Con., *Gels.*, Mag. ph.,° Nit. ac., Physos., Plumb., Ver. a.
on near vision—Graph., *Nat. m.*, *Physos.*, Rhus.

on inclining head toward shoulder—*Gels.*
laterally—Bell.
Paretic—Caust., Gels., SEN.
Spasmodic—Cic., Physos.
vertically—Bell., Nit. ac., SEN.

Distant, Objects look more, than they are—Sulph.
vision blurred—Graph., Jab., *Lil., Phos., Puls.*

Drawn together, Eyes feel, on near vision—*Merc.*

Erythropsia (sees red)—BELL., PHOS.; Calc. c., Cact., Con., Hep., Hyos., Sulph.

Field of vision reduced—Hep.

Fiery points wherever she looks—*Nat. m.*, Pic. ac.

Flickering—*Agar.*, *Ant. t.*, Bell., Calc. c., Caust., Chin. ars.,° Cycl., Graph., Ign., *Lach.*, Lyc., Phos., Sen., Sep., Sil., Sulph., Thu.; Ars., Calc. fl., Hyos.

Glimmering—Kalm.

Gray spots and serpent-like bodies—Arg. n.

Green vision (see Chloropsia).

Halo—*Bell.*, Calc. c., Lach., Os., Sep.; Amyl, Anac., Ipec., Staph., Sulph.
blue and red—Ipec.
bluish green—Os.
green—Phos., Zinc.
rainbow—*Bry.*, *Os.*, Sep.
yellow—Os.

Heat in the eye when looking—Aur., Rhod., *Ruta.*

Hemianopsia—Calc. c., Calc. s., Caust., Plumb., Sep., *Tit.*

Inferior—Aur.

Lateral—Calc. c., Morph., Mur. ac., Nat. m., Plumb.

Left—Cic.

Right—Coccul., *Lith. c., Lyc.*

Superior—*Aur., Dig.,* GELS.; Arn., Ars.

vertically—Sep., *Tit.*

Letters appear pale—Sil.

run together—Agar., Bry., Fer., Graph., Mercurial., NAT. M., Os., Physos., *Ruta,* Sil.

Light, The, seems dimmer than usual—Croc.

Muscæ volitantes—Agar., Bell., Calc. c., Carbo v., China, Chin. s., Chloral., Cimic., Cycl., Dig., Gels., Glon., Jab., Lyc., Merc., Nat. c., Nux, Phos., Sep., Sil., Sulph., Thu.; Con., Kali c., Lil., Nit. ac., Physos., Rhus.

on stooping—Glon.

Nausea on looking at moving objects—JAB.

on reading—*Jab.,* Physos.

Near objects look smaller if one eye is covered—Bell.

sighted—Agar., Carbo v., Hyos., Nit. ac., Phos., Physos.

vision difficult—Agar., BELL., Carbo v., Lach., Lyc., Merc., Phos., Sen.

disagreeable—Onos., *Ruta*, Sep.
draws the eyes—Merc., Nat. m.

Objects appear to approach and recede alternately—Cic.
crooked—Bell.
covered with rainbow colors—Bry.
shaded—Sen.
dance with each pulsation—Glon.
look bluish—Tril.
large—Nux m., Onos., Hep., Hyos.
red—Bell., *Phos.*
seem more distant than they really are—Sulph.
undulate—Bell.
waver—Con.
whirl—Pic. ac.

Photopsies (and phosphenes)—Agar., Bar. c., *Bell.*, Calc. c., Caust., Chel., Chin. s., Chloral., Cina, Croc., Cycl., Gels., Glon., Hep., Kali c., Lach., Mag. ph.,° Nat. c., *Nat. m.*, Nuph., Nux, Op., Phos., Pic. ac., Sep., Thu.

Retinal image persists—*Nat. m.*

Serpentlike bodies and gray spots—Arg. n.

Short sighted (see Near Sighted).

Sleepy on using eyes—Asa., Con., Nat. m., *Nux m.*

Small objects not seen so well as formerly—Lyc., Phos.

Spasmodic astigmia—LIL., PHYSOS.
myopia—*Jab.*, Physos.

Sudden obscuration of vision (see Vision).
Veil, A black, before the eyes—Aur. met., Phos.
Vision. Blue spots—Kali c. (see Cyanopsia).
blurs—Bell., JAB., Nat. m., *Physos.*, Sep.
changes constantly—Cic., JAB.
Colored (see Chromopsia).
confused—Aur., *Nat. m.*, Physos., Pic. ac., Puls., Rhus, Thu.
difficult—Acon., Aur. met., BELL., Lyc., *Merc.*
dim (fog, mist, veil)—Acon., Agar., Alum., Arn., Aur., Bar. c., Bell., Bry., Calc. c., Caust., Cham., Chel., China, Chin. s., Chloral., Con., Croc., Cycl., Euph., Fer., Gels., Hep., Jab., Kali b., Kali i., Lach., Lil., Lyc., Mercurial., Merc., Merc. cor., Nat. c., Nat. m., Nat. s., Nux, Onos., Os., Phos., Physos., Pic. ac., Plumb., Ran. b., Rhus, Ruta, Sang., Sec., Sen., Sep., Sil., Stram., Sulph., Thu., Tril., Zinc.; Amyl, Ars., Glon., Hyos.
green (see Chloropsia).
like hairs or feathers before the eyes—Alum.
obscuration in reading, etc.—Bell., Hep., Jab., Nat. m., Phos.
with nausea—*Jab.*, Puls.
sudden—Arg. n., Bell., Euph., *Jab.*, *Lil.*, *Nat. m.*, Nit. ac., Petr., Phos., Physos., Puls., Ruta, Stan., Sulph.
red—BELL (see Erythropsia).

unsteady—Con., Nat. m., Physos.
vanishes during a headache—Sil.; Amyl, Glon., Sang.
during menstruation—Graph., Jab., LIL., Phos., *Puls.*
on rising—Chel., China, Cina, Fer., Hep., Puls.
weak—Kali c., Nat. m., Nat. s., Phos., Physos.
Yellow (see Xanthopsia).
Waves—Bor.
White. All colors appeared—Con.
Wipe the eyes. Must—Croc., EUPH., Nat. c., Sen.
Xanthopsia (sees yellow)—CINA, *Dig.*, SANT.; Amm. c., Cycl., Hyos., Kali b.

AGGRAVATIONS.

1 to 3 a. m.—Ars., Chin. ars., Tereb.°
3 a. m.—Kali c.
10 to 11 a. m.—Cact., NAT. M.
4 to 8 p. m.—LYC.
6 p. m.—Nat. m.
After midnight—ARS., Chin. ars., *Rhus.*
Artificial light—Bell., Calc. c., Chel., Euph., Hep., *Lyc.*, Mercurial., MERC.
Change of temperature—Ars., Ran. b.
Cold—Calc. c., *Hep.*, Kali b., Kali c.

applications—*Sil.*
weather—DULC., *Ruta.*
wind—*Acon., Caust., Sep.*
Cool air—Zinc.
Damp weather—NAT. S., RAN. B., Rhus.
Dark stormy days—Kali i., Spig.
Daylight—Graph.
Evening—Acon., Alum., Ars., Ced., Chel., Cinnab., Kali b., Lyc., Merc., Nat. s., Zinc.
Toward—Lith., LYC.
Fixing the eyes—Aur. met.
Food—*Carbo v.*
Getting wet—CALC. C., RHUS.
Heat of a fire—Arg. n., Como., MERC., Nat. s.
Hot weather—Sep.°
Inner canthus—Acon., Arg. n., *Iod.*, Lyc., *Merc.*, ZINC.
Left—Agar., Bad., Ced., Chloral., Clem., Ipec., LACH., Lil., Mercurial., *Mez.*, Onos., Phyto., Sep., Sil.
Looking at a distance—*Jab.*
down—Acon., *Nat. m.*
intently at anything—*Nat. m.*
to the right—Caust.
up—Alum., Carbo v., *Chel.*
Lying down—Ced.
Morning—Acon., *Mercurial.*, Mez., Nat. ars., *Nat. m.*, NUX, Phyto., SULPH.
Motion—Acon., Arn., Ars., Aur. met., BRY.,

Caust., Chel., China, Como., Fe. ph., *Hep.*, *Jab.*, Kali b., KALM., Physos., Phyto., Prun., Sang., *Spig.*

Near vision—*Bell.*, Carbo v., Jab., Physos., Pic. ac., Rhod., *Ruta*, Sep.

Night—Aur., Bad., Cinnab., Coccul., Lyc., MERC., Nat. ars., Prun., *Tereb.*, Zinc.

Open air—Caust., Colch., Kali b., Sep., *Sulph.*

Outer canthus—Graph., Mez.

Pressure—*Aur.*, Bry., LACH., Sep.

Reflections of light—Sep.

Rest—Aur., RHUS.

Right—Agar., *Aloe*, Alum., Aur. met., *Apis*, Bry., Chel., Como., Gels., LYC., Nat. s., Paris, Prun., Ran. b., *Sil.*

Rubbing the eyes—*Sep.*, Spig.

Stooping—Coloc.

Sunlight—Acon., *Sulph.*

Touch—*Aur.*, Caust., Cham., *Hep.*, *Lach.*, Spig.

Upper lid—Acon., Alum., Apis, KALI c., Mercurial., *Mez.*, Spig.

Warm room—*Bry.*, *Pic. ac.*, PULS.

Warmth—*Arg. n.*

Water. Washing in—SULPH.

Wine—Zinc.

AMELIORATIONS.

Closing the eyes—Aur. met., Con.

Cold air—Iod., *Pic. ac.*

applications—*Pic. ac., Sec.*
Cool air—PULS.
Covering either eye—Bell.
Evening—Nat. ars.
Lacrimation—Sep.
Looking at a distance—Onos.
Lying down—Sep.
Making the eyes small—Aloe.
Motion—RHUS, Ruta.
Open air—Croc., Lil.
Pressure—*Asa.*, Coloc., Mag. ph.,° Sang.
Rainy weather—Caust.
Rest—Asa.
Rubbing—Caust., Mercurial., *Nat. c.*, Zinc.
Shading the eyes—Phos.
Stooping—Acon.
Touch—Thu.
Warm applications—*Ars.*, Mag. ph.,° *Rhus, Sil.*
room—Coloc.
Winking—EUPH.
Wiping the eyes—Bell., EUPH., Lyc.

CONDITIONS.

Air. In the open—Nat. m.
Anæmia. In—China, Chin. ars., Chin. s., Fer.
Artificial light. While reading by—Chel., Stan., Sulph.
Asthenic patient—Ant. t., *Ars.*, Calc. hy., *Carbo v., China*, Fe. ph., Gels.

Blood impaired—*Carbo v.*, Crotal., Lach., Sec.
Blowing the nose. Dim vision on—Caust.
Brain fag—*Pic. ac.*, Zinc.
Cerebrospinal debility—Coccul.
Cold air. Lacrimation in—ARS., Puls., *Sulph.*
Cold dry wind. From a—ACON., *Caust.*
Coughing. Sparks after—Nuph.
Damp warm marshy locality. From or in a—Ced.
Evening. In the—Dig., Euph., Ign., Lyc., Nat. m.
Hyperthyroidism—ARS.
Low vitality—Ars., Calc. hy., CARBO V.
Masturbation. Asthenopia from—Arg. n.,° Con.
Meal. After a—Bar. c., Nat. c., Nux.
Menstruation. During—Graph., Lil., Puls., Sep.
Morning. In the—Alum., Ant. cr., Aur., Bar. c., Bor., Caust., *Nat. m.*, Nat. s., NUX, Sang., SULPH.
Motion. Could read only while the paper was in—Bell., (Ign.?).
Night. At—Asa., Kali c., Merc.
Reading or writing. After—Croc., Lith. c.
While—Agar., Bor., Graph., Hep., Kali c., Lil., Lith. c., Mercurial., Nat. c., Rhod., Ruta, Sen.
Rheumatic gouty cases with debility—Colch.
Sexual excess. Bad effects of—Kali c., Staph.
Sthenic cases—ACON., Bell.

Storm. Just before a—Sil.
Sun. From heat of the—GLON.
Suppuration after the pus has obtained a vent—
Calc. c., SIL.
Syphilis. Mercurialized—*Hep.*, *Nit. ac.*
Tea. From too much—Spig.
Tropical countries. In—Ced.
Waking. On—LACH., Nat. c.
Water. From working in—*Calc. c.*

CHARACTERISTICS.

Acute exacerbation of chronic inflammation—
Iod.
Anguish—ACON., ARS., *Aur.*
Anxiety—ACON., ARS.
Asthenopic occipital headache—Coccul., Cimic.,
Gels., Onos.
Blondes. Fat—Calc. c., Hep.
weep easily—PULS.
Blood disorganized—*Crotal.*, Lach.
pressure high—*Bell.*
pressure low—Rad.
vessels brittle—Phos.
Borborygmus—LYC.
Burning—ARS., CARBO V.
Clock-like regularity—CED.
Cold air blowing on the eye. Sensation of—
FL. AC., Mez.

Sensitive to—Cham., Caust., Clem., HEP., SIL.
(and to cold drinks) yet > in rainy weather —Caust.
Dampness (weather or house) caused or < the condition—NAT. S.
Debility with nervous erythism—*China,* Fer.
Despair—*Ars.,* AUR.
Downward motion. Dread of—BOR.
Dread of death—*Ars.*
Drowsiness—Apis, Nux m., Op.
Dryness of mouth and throat without thirst—NUX M.
Early repletion when eating—LYC.
Excessive sensitiveness—*Cham.,* Hep., Hyper., Lach., Spig.
Exudative stage of inflammation—Kali m.°
Fanned. Wants to be—Carbo v.
Face red—BELL., Bry., Gels.
Food, Smell of, nauseates—COLCH.
Gonorrhea. Latent—NAT. S., THU.
Head, Wants, warmly wrapped—*Sil.*
Headache, Occipital, upward and settles over right eye—Sang.
Dull pains spread upward with dizziness—Onos.
Hard. Inflamed tissue is—Con., Phyto.
Heaviness—Aloe.

Hurried. Feels and walks—*Arg. n.*, Lil.

Hydrogenoid constitution (Grauvogl's)—*Nat. s.*

Indolent inflammation—*Kali b.*

Inward. Pains extend—*Aur.*

Irritable (cross, etc)—*Ant. cr.*, Ant. t., Arg. n., Aur., *Bry.*, Lil., NUX.

Mental depression—ARS., AUR., Ign., NAT. M., Puls., Rad.

Mind. Functional disturbance from overtaxing the—Nux m., Pic. ac., Zinc.

Motion, Restless aching > by continued, despite < on first moving—RHUS.

Noise. Sensitive to—Aur., Bell.

Numb, Parts feel, after the pain—Mez.

Outward. Pains extend—Asa.

Pains increase and decrease suddenly—BELL., Ced.

gradually—Stan.

like splinters or pieces of glass—*Nit. ac.*, Hep., Sulph.

radiate—Mez., *Spig.*

recur with clock-like regularity—CED.

are unbearable—CHAM.

Photophobia, and pain excessive with little or no inflammation—*Con.*

Puffy between brow and lid—KALI C.

Ravenous eater yet is thin—Iod.

Reflexes from uterus, ovaries or spine—Cimic., Cycl., Lil.

Restless rheumatism—*Rhus.*

Sleeps into an <—LACH.

Small wounds bleed much—Phos.

Storm, < on approach of a, > as soon as the rain falls—RHOD.

Sweets. Craves and is < by—*Arg. n.*

Thirst for frequent small drinks—ARS.

Thirstless, even with fever—APIS, Nux m., PULS.

Tophi—Lith. benz., Lith. c.

Ulcers without inflammation or pain—*Kali b.*
  have great pain—CON.

Unbearable. Pains or condition are—CHAM.

Vertigo—China, *Dub.*, Fer., *Gels.*, Glon., Onos., Puls.
  disappears on closing the eyes—CON.

www.ingramcontent.com/pod-product-compliance
Ingram Content Group UK Ltd.
Pitfield, Milton Keynes, MK11 3LW, UK
UKHW041226270426
12106UKWH00037B/666

9 789353 864347